Moorish American Nationality Keys

of The Moorish American Institute

Est. 1975 Œ

a Scholarly work by,

Lonnie Bray EL

ISBN 978-1-7369217-7-7

Design by Lonnie Bray EL

Published by Manuel Minder Books, LLC
Cleveland, Ohio, USA

Printed in the USA

First Print June 2, 2021

DEDICATIONS

This book is dedicated to Moorish Americans. May each find light.

This book is dedicated to the Silent Moor Masters.
May their words be heard.

This book is dedicated to the American Prophet, Noble Drew Ali.
May He be pleased with this work.

CONTENTS

PREFACE

"Moors, if you do nothing else, proclaim your nationality," for "One without a nationality is a slave in whatever nation he is found," "Study yourself and be yourself," "There should be no more secrets," "Moors and Europeans shall rise together then never fall," (Noble Drew Ali).

In Cleveland, Ohio in 1975, The Moorish American Institute was founded as an Ohio non-profit business for education by disciples of Charles Mosley Bey, disciple of Noble Drew Ali. As of 2016, The Moorish American Institute's educational programs have been motivated by Noble Drew Ali's Directives to (a) Proclaim nationality, if you do nothing else, (b) "There should be no secrets," and (c) "Moors and Europeans will rise together then never fall."

Laws are made only for humans, meaning people with lawfully-recognized nationality statuses, which is why Noble Drew Ali said, "One without a nationality is a slave in whatever nation he is found." The MAI does not want people to be slaves.

My passion for writing stems from lack of quality public and Moorish educations. A number of us Moorish American Institute graduates under the past administration concluded that MAI's course did not prepare for nationality proclamation, nor did other various Moor and Moorish organizations' programs. Therefore, we each sat out on a quest to return with a nationality education product. Such is the subject of this book.

At the time, I was in a Ph. D. program for general psychology. By the way, I entered the program to become a stronger character writer. I had no intentions of becoming a psychologist. Never the less, I inadvertently mastered the skill of scientific writing as well as a host of other skills. More important from my Ph. D. study was the fact that I gained insights to help

Moors psychologically. Within the so-called psychological world, a problem exists, which does not require keen insight in order to recognize, or to detect. The problem in the so-called psychological world, largely meaning professional American and European psychological bodies, was that there was no help for Moors. These psychological bodies continue to refuse to recognize Moors and Moorish culture, in particular, Astrology.

My dissertation argues that Astrology is a valuable tool for more well-rounded psychologists. My dissertation points to the fact that psychologists are required to possess functioning knowledge of Judeo-Christian and Islamic belief systems in order to counsel Jews, Christians, and Muslims. My dissertation argues that psychologists who counsel Moors and those from an astrological culture, and or belief system should possess a functioning knowledge of Moorish culture, or belief system, in particular, Astrology.

I presented that approximately 2 billion people, including Moors, Hindus, Indians, Chinese, Japanese, and several others are culturally, religiously, and/or psychologically tied to Astrology, and further argue that without trained psychologists schooled in Astrology, all of the above-mentioned peoples are excluded from mental health resources from the above-mentioned psychological bodies. These other psychological bodies only help those who agree to fit within their boxes.

The collective final words of my professors, counselor, advisor, head of the psych department, dean, and board were, "If you argue against Astrology, your argument will be heard." This finding meant that in order to take the next step among them, I was to dump my blood-culture as if on a roadside and walk as myself no more. I thought, Wow, these people are against me knowing myself, so they are definitely against the part of my culture that tells me to Be Myself. Therefore, I turned my thoughts toward working with, for, and by Moorish Americans.

Before taking over administration of The MAI, we founded The Moorish Psychology Association. However, first some movie producers put lumps of money into my pockets and I went to Florida, then Los Angeles to work as an actor for television and film, then to Sinaloa, México to make movies. I was having a wonderful time in places some people will only see on TV and dream about. Then near Columbia, from a beach-swim, my passport got water-damaged. The US Embassy told me they would issue a new passport to me and were kind enough to take my money for photos and passport, but then told me that they could not help me due to an arrest warrant from Cleveland, Ohio. Domestic emigration detained and extradited me to Los Angeles. I lost all of our hard-earned film equipment, cash, and the film truck. I had only jeans, t-shirt, shoes, hoodie, underwear, less than $2,000 US, and two ounces of silver.

In the Los Angeles penal system, which can be both jail and prison, jail for me, I was mistaken for a Black and locked up with only Blacks. I was mistaken for a Mexican and locked up with only Mexicans, Norteños, Soreños, and Pizanos. Norteños are Northern California Mexicans, Soreños are Southern California Mexicans, and Pizanos are Mexicans from México. Though the LA penal system labels Norteños and Soreños collectively as Homies, Norteños and Soreños do not like each other. Pizanos do not like Norteños, or Soreños. Separated from sun and real food, I lost weight and became so pale that I was labeled, "Wood," which in the LA penal system means, "White." I was locked up as in a white man in a caged area with only whites.

The Mexicans and Whites did not like each other. However, undetected among them all, I got to hear what they all thought of the Blacks. They all spoke respectfully when they said they would not want to be Black, not because of skin color, or any other reason that one may think, but simply because Blacks have no, what is called, "Program." On the other hand, Mexicans and Whites do have programs, which means they eat, study, exercise, and pray together. Also, Whites and Mexicans included each other and confided in one another, whereas Blacks had no such programs for growth, or even support. No organization, no plan. On this point I agreed with the Mexicans and Whites.

In the open, after Blacks, Woods, Norteños, Sureños, and Pizanos all knew full-well who I am, they took turns inviting me to sit at their tables for them only. They all offered food to me and I ate with them all. In confirmation that they meant no racial disrespect against Blacks, they all said to me about Blacks what they had said when they thought their conversation private, which is, "The problem with Blacks is that they have no program."

With unity and clarity of self and common identity, Mexicans and Whites find inter-group communications possible. However, inter-group communications where Blacks are involved are extra complicated and difficult, because Blacks have no united group. Blacks are so divided that a word, or token of respect with one may to another be a deadly offense. For examples, a Black may, or may not also claim to be a Negro, a Colored, a Person of Color, an Afro-American, an African American, African, or Indian.

Legal systems forced me to learn to think and to write for criminal and civil procedures. In courts I got to exercise my knowledge, wear my fes, and demonstrate as a Moor defending myself and I won. While I was held captive, the past MAI Headmaster made transition, as Moorish

Americans say in place of passed, or died. Months later, after I won the legal battles, a group of MAI alumni came to my home and suggested that I should be the new Headmaster. I was at the time managing The Moorish Psychology Association and operating The Sultanate Of Erie Office as acting Sultan and happy with a developing education program for nationality proclamation and I did not want more responsibility. However, after seeing those Moors' enthusiasm, drive, and commitment, I agreed to work as Headmaster and to fulfill the duties of an MAI vice-president.

Today, I am Headmaster of The MAI and CEO and my intentions are to present only academia as academia. This work should clear up confusion concerning what Moorish American Nationality is and how to establish Moorish American Nationality. I have become fully aware of the two most important reasons for so much confusion concerning Moorish American Nationality and the process of proclaiming such. Those reasons are incompetence and crime in the forms of religious cult leaders, scam artists, and outright thieves who are sometimes not even proclaimed Moorish Americans.

In pursuit of a lawful status correction process that establishes Moorish American Nationality, my family, friends, and I exchanged thousands of US notes. Yet, we received only confusion, non-sense, and no follow-up. Some even had identities stolen. Hustlers have altered, rearranged, re-purposed, and repackaged Charles Mosley Bey's works, Clock of Destiny 1, Clock of Destiny 2, and The Zodiac Constitution. We know, because the originals were handed to us. With minimal educations and false educations, hustlers and thieves have led my people astray.

My lessons came via sweat, blood, tears, time, cash, humiliation, loss, and grief. Never the less, I am proud to say that all of my teachers who had a say in what I do with information imparted to me related that, "You may do whatever you want with the information." I have walked the path of Moorish American methodology and defended it in state and federal courts. Such are now all matters of public record. I invite you to utilize these lessons as measuring rods and strengths to stand upon.

Throughout key parts of my education, had it not been for Europeans, German, Irish, Italian, Russian, and Polish, I would not have been able to take the next step. It makes absolutely no sense to point at a pale helping-hand and say, Enemy, when so many proven enemy-hands have been and are brown and in the temples and other Moorish American organizations collecting green; yet, offering only darkness.

The Moorish Psychology Association

The Moorish Psychology Association is an association of psychologists trained in the methods of Lonnie Bray EL in order to deal with the psychological issues of Moorish Americans. Our Mission Statement is *The More I know, The More I Can Help*. Moorish Psychologists are Humanists. We believe that under the stars, all people are equal and we study and learn about Humans from Humans, not white rats, monkeys, or dogs. Moorish psychotherapy is designed to get one to know one's self, so that one may be one's self in all walks of life and with honor.

Knowing self strengthens resolve, confidence, and community as well as establishes legal competence. One who does not know self is legally incompetent, mentally unstable, and may at best function, judge, and decide only through another's morals. When the setting is law and the subject is nationality, legal incompetence, by default, forces one into Property Status, meaning, Property of some government. Property cannot own property, or defend self in law.

The Moorish Psychology Association is committed to Psychological Health and Accountability through one-to-one care, confidentiality, education, nutrition, exercise, and learning how others learn. Moorish Psychology argues that Moorish psychology, history, and culture are tools that help build psychological strengths and defenses for All. As well, Moorish Psychology advocates for other older as well as newer mainstream psychological approaches, for examples, Mesmoorism/Mesmerism, Poetry Therapy, and Movie Therapy.

The Sultanate Of Erie

The Sultanate Of Erie was founded in accord with The Moorish Divine And National Movement as an Indigenous American government operating in the Erie region for the express purpose of assisting with Nationality proclamations, records protection, and verification.

The Sultanate Of Erie proudly constructs, protects, verifies, and replaces Nationality Documents, provides nationality education, cultural education, legal support, and psychological support in partnership with The MAI and The Moorish Psychology Association.

INTRODUCTION

Take Your Moorish American Education to The Next Level

Races

Races are 'stateless,' non-Human identities, not demanding Lawful Respect. Nationality is Human identity and attached with Blood, Land, Flag, Ancestral Religion, Ancestral Name, and Lawful Respect. No Nations, Lands, Flags, or Religions are named Black, White, Brown, Red, or Yellow, so neither should Humans.

    Those who identify as non-Humans cause perpetual psychological, social, and economic troubles. They cause psychological troubles, because they do not know who they are, so neither can others. They cause social troubles by being excluded from international conversations and culture. They may cause economic troubles, because business people may not to do business with stateless people.

What is <u>Moorish American Nationality Keys Of The Moorish American Institute</u>?

Moorish American Nationality Keys Of The Moorish American Institute is Key to returning Human-Identity with Blood, Land, Flag, Ancestral Name, Ancestral Religion, Dignity, and Respect in Law through the National Identity, "Moor, a term replaced with negro, for purposes of slavery" (Johnson, 1775). A source of information for Administrative Law - Indigenous Peoples and Court Records Procedures dealing with Moorish American Nationality Proclamation, Status Change, and a Right-Of-Passage.

Moorish American Nationality Keys Of The Moorish American Institute is Moorish American Education Facts on Moorish American History, Moorish American Culture, Moorish Psychology, Moorish Science, Math, and Law. Enables Moorish thinking, dressing, and living. An inexpensive, time-effective, start-to-finish guide from a credible source, backed by war-education and International War-Records, demanding more accurate accounting than Public Education.

What does <u>Moorish American Nationality Keys Of The Moorish American Institute</u> do?

Moorish American Nationality Keys Of The Moorish American Institute gives Answers to the questions, How do I claim my Nationality? What do Moorish Americans teach? and Do I have to be religious to be Moorish American?

Moorish American Nationality Keys Of The Moorish American Institute Builds awareness and administrative capacity for Civil Registry and Helps eliminate discrimination and gaps in National Laws causing statelessness, in alliance with goals of The United States Department Of State (https://www.state.gov/other-policy-issues/statelessness/#). Stops bullying by law enforcement.

Moorish American Nationality Keys Of The Moorish American Institute Enables Moorish Thinking, Dressing, and Living through Moorish American Education Facts on Moorish American History, Moorish American Culture, Moorish Psychology, Moorish Science, Math, and Law.

Who is <u>Moorish American Nationality Keys Of The Moorish American Institute</u> for?

Moorish American Nationality Keys Of The Moorish American Institute is **F**oundational for Moorish Education Courses, Moorish American Education Degrees, online schools for Moors, and Moorish Consulates; **a must for** those who want respectable education delivered simple and fast and to be taken seriously about the subject of Moors, Respectors and Lovers of Moors and Moorish Culture, as well as Indigenous Peoples and plain 'ol Black folks who just want to know where they come from.

Market research shows that People purchase the *Moorish American Nationality Keys Of The Moorish American Institute* for reasons such as in order to say, "Here's my proof." Some are looking for ways to strengthen senses of togetherness, not separation. Some want new ideas for content, or art. Some want to become part of an intellectually elite circle. Some need help calming a troubled child, or enabling one. Some may be students of History, Archeology, Anthropology, or Social Sciences looking for an edge in grades and some want to grow their minds alone for now, while others are seeking to bring teacher's fallacies into the light. Another reason market research also shows that readers tend to trust the text more, because author is a man of both academic and physical integrity.

Who is <u>Moorish American Nationality Keys Of The Moorish American Institute</u> not for?

Moorish American Nationality Keys Of The Moorish American Institute is not for those looking for religious support, superiority support, or other ways to divide Humans, avoid taxes, commit crimes with impunity, or unnecessarily enter courtrooms as Defendant.

About <u>Moorish American Nationality Keys Of The Moorish American Institute</u>

In Law, Laws are for humans, Humans have nationalities, and men, women, and children without a Nationality are lawful Government Property. Human and Property Statuses are choices. This work is strengthened by war-education and International War-Records, which unlike public educations, demand more accurate accounting.

Moorish Americans, do you feel that you have been lied to and tricked as if by wolves in sheep's clothing? Have you been offered a complicated process for an excessive amount of money and did not receive what you thought you would? This book provides a simple path and an inexpensive solution to a goal, is from a credible academic source, and will guide the reader all the way.

With my permission, portions of this work are from <u>The Book Of Moors</u>. <u>The Book Of Moors</u> premise is that the sounds, Ali, EL, Bey, and of course Moor, are Imperial Keys to decoding and comprehending Moors as a nation of people belonging to a global and truly ancient Empire connected through Old Order ISLAM, Math, Astrology, The Self Law of I, Buddhism, The Golden Order Of Kongfu, and more (TheMoorishAmericanInstitute.org). A portion of this work began as undergraduate psychology lectures, which I designed in order to prepare psychologists to face natural psychological problems arising within a man, woman, or child absent of the concept of national identity. Another portion of this work is inspired by the education of my grandfather, Grandmaster Marvin Bray EL 33 1/3°, 1886-1992.

Crusades   To describe some relations in a curt paragraph: There were wars, which Moors call Invasions and Christians describe as Holy Wars and Crusades, times when Christians made sacred pacts, gave holy oaths, and promised to invade Moor lands, what Christians call Holy Lands, and kill as many Moors as they can and steal as much from Moors as they can in exchange for a share of the take and Church forgiveness for the sins of murder, theft, and rape. Christian leaders, including US presidents into the 1990s have declared Crusades. The overall Christian-told Crusade story is neatly packaged as wars between pale European Christians and Moors, with pale Europeans invading Africa, Asia, and America after first gaining independence from Moors in Europe. Yet, in reality, such packaging is false, because Church agents, including soldiers, knights, generals, treasurers, priests, bishops, arch bishops, and even Popes were, and are sometimes Moors. Also necessary to take into consideration is that sometimes Christians fought for Moors. Crusades continue to this day perpetrated not just by armed pale secret society members killing in, for, and with Christian armies and navies and in cruisers, but also by armed and unarmed Moor Christian secret society members, which makes identifying an enemy based on physical appearance; e.g., skin, hair, or eye color, impossible.

Crusades also continue through educational war. In 1863 Cc, USA libraries, public schools, and institutions of higher learning eliminated

Moorish history and related subjects. Moorish History became educational tools reserved for secret society members in order to learn the nature and glue of the power system in place and how to function and rise within such. Such practices continue to contribute to disenfranchising, subjecting, and enslaving Indigenous peoples in their own lands.

Commonly, European men were raised to degrees in order to be caretakers and key-holders for Indigenous Moors until the time of Moorish slavery in America was over. Instead those men became Christian agents, then Christianized, meaning fictionalized, history. Then they made education mandatory. Such public systems hypnotize, control minds, and cast people into intellectual darkness. Yet, simple keys do shed light and several are herein.

Reportedly, most legislatures, politicians, enforcers, higher education administrators, and business heads, for examples, are secret society members. They recognize one another with unauthorized Moorish titles and with honorary Christian knight titles. They have full knowledge of Moor Peoples, The Moor Empire and history, and Moorish science. Secretly, they practice Moorish culture. Openly, they are forbidden to discuss anything dealing with Moors with neighbors, friends, or even with family. I am not bound to silence by secret oaths, obligations, or morals. I never promised to hide. The education I present is of my culture, so I have right to share as I deem. I deem that sharing fosters growth, strength, and familiarity, which helps to eliminate fear and achieve Human Status for All.

A Note For Secret Society Members

For the reasons above, learned Moors affirm to not teach secret society members.

Escaping Secret Societies.   Escaping a secret society the Moor way requires enduring a sacred ceremony known as <u>The Praying Out Ceremony</u>. <u>The Praying Out Ceremony</u> nullifies contracts made by people without a lawfully-established nationality, because one without a lawfully-established nationality does not know self and is, therefore, lawfully incompetent to enter into contracts. Contracts include oaths, vows, and pledges. Enduring the <u>Praying Out Ceremony</u> is mandatory before Nationality Proclamation.

A Moorish Code is, One must be raised from a dead level to a living perpendicular. This means that property, cattle property, a person without a nationality, must be raised to human status. Such is a wonderful thought;

however, reality is that some cattle property learns, but does not raise self, preferring instead to remain cattle property. Never the less, Knowledge, in code referred to as Light, is the Justice that raises one, that saves one's self.

OTHER WORKS BY SAME AUTHOR

The Book Of Moors, The Moor Rite Volume 1, Moor People Meaning and Military.
(2023), Bowker: USA.

The Book Of Moors, The Moor Rite Volume 2, Moors Civilizers Others Civilized
(2024), Bowker: USA.

*The Book Of Moors, The Moor Rite Volume 3, Beautiful Culture Hidden and
Forbidden* (2024), Bowker: USA.

*The Book Of Moors, The Moor Rite Volume 4, Moors of the West, an honorable
argument for True Blood Americans utilizing the national terms, Moor and
Moorish American, and Spotlighting Historic Enemies (2024).* Bowker: USA.

TERMS

i.e.   that is.

e.g.   for example.

viz.   namely.

Mc   Moor Calendar. [A simple way to calculate the Moor calendar is subtract 580 years from the Christian calendar (Cc)].

Cc   Christian calendar.

BCc   Before the Christian calendar.

b. c.   born circa (near).

Christianize, Romanticize, and **Anglicize**   all mean **Fictionalize**.

S and Z.   Where there is a choice between S and Z, we prefer Latin S, as in Fes, as opposed to the Christian addition to the Latin characters, Z, as Z is unnecessary.

If I have erred, please correct me.

This publication is presented in cooperation with The Sultanate Of Erie, The Moorish Psychology Association, The Moorish Science Temple Of America, Temple Da Moor, Family, and Friends.

Chapter 1

Nationality
Citizenship Status
America

NATIONALITY

Nationality is a matter of international law and required for full citizenship in any country, or nation-state. Nationality requires recognition with the Five Human Elements, which are Blood, Land, Flag, Free National Appellation, and Ancestral Religion.

Nationals

Nationals are people belonging to a particular Nation by origin, birth, blood, and/or allegiance who share traditions.

We examine Nationality and Citizenship together, from which one should come to comprehend that (a) Not every citizen has a nationality, (b) Nationality proclamation is only one of several steps required in

International Law in order to correct status to Human, and (c) the power of the Moorish American Nationality combined with the Non-US Citizen National Status creates Human recognition in International Law.

State

A state is a governing body in the minds of People. A State has jurisdiction over the National and the National enjoys the protection and benefits of the state.

Allegiance and Jurisdiction

Allegiance and Jurisdiction identifies a bond between a National and a Nation State. (More on Nationals p 3).

Key differences between Moorish American and Moor American Nationalities

Both Moorish American and Moor American are honorable nationality identifiers. However, one, Moorish American, has the advantage of being already established as an Indigenous American national identity with an ancestral religion. We, Indigenous Americans from several backgrounds, surnames, clans, and families; e.g., Blackfoot, Leni Lenape, Kata (Choktaw), Seminole, and Tsalaki (Cherokee), have accepted Noble Drew Ali as our prophet. For legal defenses at least, one may need a prophet. Alas, we Moorish Americans have a prophet. On the other hand, in order to complete the nationality process with Indigenous American recognition; yet, without Noble Drew Ali's platform, one has the extra challenge of explaining and describing Ancestral Religion.

Free to Proclaim Nationality

Prophet Noble Drew Ali related that proclaiming nationality is free, meaning that there should be no additional charge for conducting the nationality proclamation ceremony and stamping a document. However, if one does not possess all of the required education, skills, and resources needed, and needs another to do the work, then the worker is worthy of wage. The wage should be no more than the fee for a driver's license. The fee is merely to cover expenses and an opportunity to show a token of respect, not to enrich the worker, but to enrich The Moorish American Nation by a new human joining.

As well, in order to acquire official documents, someone must pay for printing, paper, ink, photos, mailings, office filings, electricity, phone calls, official document copies, maybe travel, and official document fees, which make up the bulk of all fees and are not paid to a Moorish office. Lastly, Indigenous Nationality Proclamation requires connection to an Indigenous American government as ceremony conductor, document provider, and records protector and verifier. In order to show government support and maintain good standing within one's own government as well as others who may inquire, dues need to be paid. Minimal dues of $12 per year should be fine.

If there is no local Indigenous government office near, then perhaps one should consider gathering a few others and beginning a new local government. This book may help.

Nationality can never be taken away from the Indigenous, or judged. Yet, a citizenship status may be altered for punishment, or relinquishment, knowingly, or unknowingly, for examples. The rest of the citizenship lecture is reserved for the next section.

Nationality Document Part 1

The Nationality Document is the foundation for achieving Human Status in Law. Only one page, the first page, the Nationality Certificate, needs to be presented for proof of nationality, or naturalization, depending on status, because such bears witness to allegiance. Such is not just true for Moorish Americans, but of all nations and governments which I have researched and I have researched nations on all continents with nations.

The second page should provide personal statistics and information linking one to and describing The Moor Nation and government, as well as the words of the actual Word of Allegiance. The third and final page is the signature page, making a document total of three pages. Such is neat, curt, and all Law requires for argument and favorable finding, and with fewer pages to argue over, or to have challenged.

Fees for constructing a nationality document should be minimal. A sincere Moorish American government, meaning one focused on fostering growth in the Moorish American Nation, should without fee and cheerfully construct a nationality document for one unable to pay, and require no more than one's word of honor to pay later. Hands, backs, and minds working for the nation is worth more than nationality document fees.

With a proper nationality document in-hand, one has a solid foundation on which to build and may then assert one's self and gain government-recognition of Rights and travel without hassle. Before one takes the next step with the <u>Nationality Document</u>, one must have command knowledge of citizenship and citizenship statuses.

CITIZENSHIP

Citizenship is a state political term synonymous with Class and government-recognition of civil, political, and social rights, responsibilities, and privileges, such as ability to work for a government and get elected to office, or lack thereof.

Each state is free to create citizenship and citizenship removal laws. Thus, in some Nations, nationality and citizenship are sometimes the same. For examples, Jewish citizens of Israel are Jewish Nationals, Arab citizens of Israel are Arab Nationals; yet, neither are Israeli. In Liberia only those of, "Black African origins," may be citizens. Spain's citizens have several Nationalities; e.g., Andalusian, Aragonese, Balearic, and Galician. Kurds have never had land, yet, claim Kurdish Nationality and Kurds may be joined. For another example of national identifiers, early Soviets identified Nationality by factors such as language, religion, and clothes.

Citizenship Statuses

There are five basic citizenship statuses. Within each Nation, Citizen is the highest and there are more than one type of citizen.

First to be Classed Citizens - Nationals. Nationals are a government's first to be classed citizens; i.e., the oldest, or first people on a land, the Indigenous People with blood rights, called **Jus Sanguinis Rights**, which are Ancestral Land Rights. First to be Classed Citizens are sometimes mistakenly referred to as First-Class Citizens.

For ease of life-navigation, certain identifications may describe a Moorish American's, or an American Moor's national, or citizenship status simply as, **American National** and **American Citizen** (a good thing and different than US Citizen, see below). First to be Classed Citizens may contribute to federal campaign funds and hold federal office; yet, are non-tax obligated to the US government and may not be deported.

Some of America's First to be Classed Citizens are Moorish Americans, "the copper-colored natives found in America by the pale Europeans (Noah Webster, *American Dictionary of the English Language*, 1828). Copper is the metal of the US Of A's basic coin, the penny, because America's nobles have copper-like skin. [Interestingly, the penny bares the image of Abraham Lincoln, credited with freeing "the slaves." Lincoln is said to be the son of a Melungeon woman, i.e., a dark skin person of mixed Moor and pale European stock from Tennessee Country, according to *Webster's Comprehensive Dictionary Of The English Language, The New International, Encyclopedic Edition, p. 794* (2006).

Second to be Classed Citizens - Naturals. A nation, or government's Second to be classed citizens are **Natural Citizens**, also known as **Naturalized Citizens**. These are former **Alien Nationals**, meaning a national from another nation, who has fulfilled the requirements for citizenship with a new nationality within a new nation, called the naturalization process. The term, "**Naturalization**," means, The conferring of nationality and/or citizenship of a state upon a human after birth, by any means whatsoever. Second to be Classed Citizens may contribute to federal campaign funds. Both First and Second to be Classed Citizens are equal Citizens in the eyes of the law. Yet, Natural Citizens may have citizenship revoked and be deported for punishment of crime.

Children of naturalized people born in the new country have **Jus Soli** (pronounced Yoos Olee) Birth Rights, Rights to benefit from labor on the land. This includes Moors born in America, who claim African origins. For examples, Moor Americans, **Mooroons** of Jamaica, Haiti, and ancestors of Nyanga, in Yanga, Veracruz, México.

Third to be Classed Citizens - Aliens. Third to be Classed Citizens are **Aliens**, people from another nation without citizenship, or Permanent Resident Status, in which one is. These may include stateless people and is a temporary citizenship status for privileges related to work and education, for examples. Aliens may not contribute to federal campaign funds.

Alien and **Foreign National** are the same term in law. US Immigration Law uses the term, Alien. Political rules use the term Foreign National.

Permanent Resident. also legally and lawfully recorded as *Resident, Permanent Resident Alien, Lawful Permanent Resident, Resident Alien Permit-holder*, and *Greencard-holder*, is the highest US Alien citizenship status for immigrants. Permanent Residents have the rights to (a) permanently reside and work in a country, (b) hold local office, and (c) petition for family member's citizenship. Yet, not vote in federal elections, or hold federal office. Like Citizens, Permanent Residents may live, work, and study on the land, receive social benefits, protection, and must pay taxes permanently in most circumstances.

Exceptions are Moorish Americans who construct their documents so that they remain indigenous to the land, America; yet, Alien to the US government. Such is not our path; yet, also provides freedom from corporate slavery, deportation, and unlawful taxes.

Resident Aliens.   are visa-holders with the right to temporarily reside, work, and/or study in a country, but are not citizens, may not hold office, or vote, and must pay taxes on all income.

Non-resident Aliens   may be Student Visa-holders or Work Visa-holders permitted to study, or to work, and may be required to pay taxes on income earned within a country.

Fourth to be Classed - Subjects.   The Fourth to be Classed Status, Subject, is not a citizenship status, but the mark of a government's lawful property, called **Cattle Property**. Subjects/Property may indeed enjoy privileges, yet, not Rights, because they are without a stated allegiance, national claim, or a nation to claim them. Subjects/Property are citizens of nowhere. Therefore, they may be lawfully treated inhumanely and may not own property. Such is why most land and transport deeds are not owner's deeds.

Property/Subject classifications are, for examples, Black, White, Negro, Colored Person, Person of Color, Indian, African American, Asian, Pacific Islander, and Puerto Rican. **Puerto Rico** is a common wealth of the US government; yet, is not and never was a Nation. (See Borinken Moors and Taíno Moors p. 7).

Fifth to be Classed - Undesirables.   The Fifth to be Classed are not citizens, or non-citizens, but Undesirables, people whom a national government wants deported.

American Citizen

By law, the term, American Citizen, identifies Indigenous Americans; i.e., Moors.

US Citizen

By law, "Citizen of the US is different than Citizen of one of the several states," and "US Citizen is a special class of citizen created by congress," (US v. Anthony 24 Fed. 829, 1873). The citizenship status of a US Citizen is Subject, regardless of Black, or White, because neither Black nor White are nationalities, never were, and there has never been a Black, or White land, flag, language, or religion to represent a Blood Nation of People.

United States is different than United States Of America

United States is different than United States Of America. Therefore, US government and US Citizen are different than US Of A government and US Of A Citizen and True American Citizen.

What Does US Mean?   US means United States.

What is the US?   "United States means a federal corporation," according to <u>28 United States Code (USC) subsection 3002 15(A)</u>.

Where is the US?   "The United States is located in the District of Columbia," <u>(USC 9-307)</u>, which is merely a ten-mile radius of land. Most people born in America were not born within the US; i.e., the District of Columbia. It is advantageous for governments to gain citizens. However, if one is like most people, including me, not born in the US, then one is not a Citizen of the US corporation.

By the way, Columbia was first called New Granada in honor of the last Moor European Sultanate, ruled by Sultan Mohammed 12th Nasr Ali.

Citizen of the United States Of America

Citizen of the United States, or US Of A Citizen, is a law term authorized by <u>The Constitution for The United States Of America</u>, which was authorized by The Moor Empire through Sultan Tsidi Mohammed 3rd Bey of Moorocco. A Citizen of one of the several states is a US Of A Citizen. Why? Because, US Of A Citizens were born within a state republik, or territory, but not within the United States, again meaning, Washington District of Columbia.

What then is the United States Of America?

The United States Of America is all of the states united in cooperation outside of and exclusive of the area known as the United States; i.e., the District of Columbia.

WARNING: SOVEREIGN CITIZEN MOVEMENT

A Human's State is The State of Self, which must not be confused with the Sovereign Citizen Movement, a pale European American movement based on a strategy to claim American Land Labor Rights through a process of expatriating from the US, then going through the US's naturalization process as originating from a European land and blood, but born in America. The fact that Indigenous is a Nation's highest status means that an Indigenous claim is above any claim, including that of the sovereign citizen movement. In actuality, a Nation's Sovereign is the one who controls that nation's gold. Thus, there are no sovereign citizens, which is why the US federal government has labeled Sovereign Citizens as, "Terrorists," paper terrorists, yet, terrorist none the same and just as threatening as any agency wants to portray them. Moors working in this movement are in dishonor for trying to help others usurp Moorlands.

INTRODUCTION
to

CHAPTER 2

The path is only complicated, because wicked people make simple things seem complex.

Respect

Respect is the honorable path to everything in life. Respect is due to Moors and to Moor warriors. Moor culture is a culture based both on love, as one may gather from Chapter 3; yet, a feudal culture physically held together mostly by Beys and the Bey-trained. Therefore, before showing the Love-Face of Moor culture, I stick with the Moorish tradition of first showing the War-Face. Such comes from the Strangers Greeting Ceremony with the Mask of Seth. Historically, warriors are records keepers. Traditionally, Beys compose the bulk of Moorish militaries world-wide. This chapter partly demonstrates Moors in Africa and Asia. It is always important to show and to approach a new culture with respect. Therefore, know this:

Africa

Africa is a continent, not a nation. Africa has no Flag, Language, or GOD. The Moor Empire on African soil was ruled by several sub-rulers. There are not, nor has there ever been, distinct peoples known nationally as Africans.

Tsong Hua 中国 China Chinese

Tsong Hua 中国 is to Christians, *China* and *Chino*. **Tsongwen** 中文 **Of Tsong** is to Christians, *Chinese*. **Tsong Hua Rén** 中国人 is to Christians, *Chinese People*. China, Chino, and Chinese are 16th century Cc Christian designations for China, Taiwan, Manchuria, Inner Mongolia, Xinjiang, and Tibet. The people whom Christianized, Anglicized, and westernized-thought refers to as, "Chinese people," do not refer to themselves as Chinese people and there is no such land as China. The people whom Anglicized-thought refers to as Chinese people refer to their land as **Tsong Hua** and to themselves as **Tsong Hua Rén, the people of Tsong Hua.**

From what I am told, in Christian-ruled countries, several Tsonghua Rén people pretend to be Chinese due to resistance to education, as Christian educators simply re-label anyone and anything without regard for dignity, or honor. The threat for non-compliance is deportation. There is no China; however, there is Bey, what the West knows as Northern China, and places such as Hebey, Hubey, and Beyjing, The Capitol City, for examples. In fact, the entire land that the West identifies as China was all once ruled by very dark Moors and to this day, is still ruled by Moors, from a Moor's perspective.

Nihon Nihonjin Japan Japanese

There is no such thing as Japan, or Japanese people. Those people refer to themselves as Nihonjin and to their land as Nihon. Nihon's traditional government-rule and individual Samoorai house-hold-rule is called Beykufu. Samoorai are those who serve the Moor nobles. Shogun and Daimiyo are Christian terms never in use by Beykufu, Samoorai, or Nihonjin.

CHAPTER 2

MOOR MILITARY

FOREVER MORE
WE'LL DANCE OR WAR
OR WHATEVER THE PARTY'S FOR
SO LONG AS THE PARTY REMAINS
FOREVER MOOR.

Party *n* 1. a gathering of people for war. 2. a social gathering for fun.

Theater *n* 1. the location of war. 2. places of entertainment; for plays, ballets, and orchestras.

Stage *n* **1.** the location of battle. **2.** the entertainment area of a theater.

Military *n* things of Aries; i.e., war.

11

Moor Military Titles

Moor Culture is a feudal culture, meaning it functions off war and war principles, such as, mostly respect and laws and guideless of how to reward the respectful and punish the disrespectful. Below are military titles and other military information concerning Moors.

Ali.   a hereditary title and Top Officer of a Nation, meaning Master and Most High.

EL.   a hereditary title and Top Officer in the field, or theater, with derivative titles Mooroshel/Marshal, General, and Admiral.

Mooroshel/مارشال.   *The Supreme Imperial General* And *Admiral*, *The/El* of All military forces of one organization under the Executive. The Christianized version is *Marshal*. **Martial** in Arabic, يركسع, renders the sound, *Iskree*. Marshal and Martial are tied.

Bey.   a hereditary title type of general ruling in wartime and peace time.

(More on Ali, EL, and Bey in ᗱꞣꞟ ᗷꝋꝋꝁ Ꝋꝼ ᗰꝋꝋᚱꙄ).

Emir/Amir.   a type of general, or Prince in Christian terminology. There are also **Lieutenant-Emirs**, and **Major-Emirs** like lieutenant general and major general.

Khan.   Khan, borrowed from and in honor of The Khanan [Canaan] Empire, is the title of a type of Imperial Moor General charged to Khanquest [conquest] and to Khanquer [Conquer]. Khans warred with one another, all trying to become **The One Great Khan**, contributing to the Moor Empire's fall.

Aga Khan.   Moslem hereditary military title given to the heads of the Families Of Ali.

Victor.   A Moorish general rank of Rome. For example, the Moor, **Saint Victor I r. 189-199 Cc**, who had been Bishop Victor of Rome, born in Tripoli, Africa and morphed His state language to Latin as did other Moor governments in Africa, America, El Andalus, and other parts of

Europe.

Kaesar.   Kaesar, Caesar, and Kzar are ways to say, Roman Emperor.

Standard Ranks.   All hold the Moor traditional offices, Moorshal/ Marshal, General/Admiral, Colonel, Major, Captain, and Lieutenant with enlisted ranks, Sergeant, Corporal, Private.

Moor Warrior Proficiencies.   Each Moor Warrior is traditionally required to be proficient in hand-to-hand combat, horse-riding, archery, swimming, and basic medicine.

Allies.   Moor warriors and accepted Moors in league with the sovereign, Ali

Aligents/Allegeance.   Non-Moors in service to a Moor sovereign.

Troopers.   Imperial combatants.

Soldiers.   a slave rank, one sold, or who sells one's self into service.

Mujahideen (Holy Warriors), **Muslema/Musalemat**, **Yainissary**, and **Slavs** are slave advanced infantry Orders key to The Moor Empire's military.

Yahyah.   Infantry.

Mubarizun.   Highly conditioned infantry, who strategize to weaken enemy moral.

Sharif | Sheriff | Shareef.   a high law-enforcer, who descends from Prophet Mohammed's bloodline and has the power to appoint deputies and to call and command a military called The Militia.

Militia.   fighters under **Millet**; i.e., **Moorish Law** and **Moslem Customary Law**.

Moorines.   Moorines, or House Moorine [Marines to Christians], are traditionally Hashshashyn Bey Special Forces Families living by the Moorine Code, *Simper Fidelis: Honor Above All Else Except Loyalty*. House Moorine gave their title to become honored as the identity of a special military force operable on land, sea, and air, regardless of blood connection, or religion. By tradition, one who joins The Moorines takes Moorine as one's permanent identity, and is accepted as family. Moorines are traditionally armed with a Crescent Moon Sword, [primary weapon, also known as **Scimitar, Shamshir, Mamaluke**, and others] a **Da Moor Sword** [also known as **Dragon Sword**], a sword similar to the Roman Gladius, straight, double-bladed, and short [primarily for assassination], maybe a small buckler shield attached on a forearm, and heavily armed with light weapons including a spear, light javelins, a Crescent knife, daggers, darts, picks, needles, and later, pistols, rifles, and more.

Mounties. Imperially specialized land-forces composed of man and stead, horse, kamel, or elephant. *Mountie* relates to *mountain, mount,* and to *mounting,* and means *To command self, stead, and mountain in a triangle relationship of respect*; i.e., give and take. Mounties may command Troopers, Troops, and Soldiers. *Rukban* are specifically Kamelback Mounties. Mountie traditional arms are the Crescent Moon Sword and Da Moor Sword, both for battling and dueling; a short sword similar to the Roman Gladius [primarily as a battle backup], Crescent knife [to skin game, survive, or kill, lance, a few spears, light javelins, maybe a buckler shield attached on a forearm, then later, pistols, rifles, and more.

Mounties And Moorines. Navigators guided by the North Pole Star and the first armored, mounted, saddled, and spurred warriors.

Marines represent LAW; i.e., Love, Art, and War and their mechanisms, quality, refinement, and **Eloquence**, **Elegance**'s essence, which is expressed *Christianized*, *Romanticized*, and *Anglicized* as **Chivalry**; i.e., things of **Calvary**, and **Cavalry**.

Bey Moors are Moors of legend living a noble culture of wits in love and war, delivering prizes, poems, and sweets to lovers, and loving like there is no tomorrow.

Romance and *Romantic* have nothing to do with Amoor/Love.

Some Mounties and Moorines noble and Yainissary, became **Knights**, meaning Moor Empire traders and members of Christian soldier Orders, or **Gentlemen** Orders such as **Soldiers For JESUS CHRIST And Mary, Soldiers For Father Son And Holy Ghost**, and **Dragon**, from where such men are classically depicted as tall, dark, and handsome in shining armor.

Gentileman, Gentleman, and **Gentile** mean **Heathen**, *one of an uncovenanted nation not knowing the true God* (McAdam and Milne, 1963. p 195); whereas *Gentilism* and *Gentility* mean *heathenism and paganism* (p

95).

Samoorai [Samurai] 侍.　The Samoorai, meaning *Moor Warrior Servants*, are Moor Families living by The Samoorai Code: *Honor Above All Else Except Loyalty*. Samoorai used THE BUDDHA DA MOOR BEY's Buddhism to formulate **The Bushido Codes**, which became **The Way of The Samoorai** and **Zen**, which translates to, *The Self-Law of I*.

In the sixth century Cc, Moorman **Beykje** [Baekje] introduced Buddhism to **Nihon** [Japan to Christians]. In the 12ᵗʰ century Cc, Moorman, **Eisai Bey**, of **The Chan Lingji Buddhism Martial School** introduced THE BUDDHA DA MOOR BEY's Buddhism to Nihon.

Translating from the Nihongo language [Japanese to Christians], there exists no differences between Moor and Mur, as in Samurai and Samoorai, the warrior class of Nihon. Samoorai is 侍 and sounds, *Sam Moor I*.

Talaiah.　Talaiah are Moorish spies.

Nahab El Muon.　hunter/foragers.

Moorcenaries.　Fighters for hire.

Musketeers.　Foot artillery. Some eventually went to work as primary bodyguards for the French Crown. **Alexandre Dumas 1804-70 Cc** is the Moor Frenchman, who wrote the classic novel, *The Three Musketeers*.

Hashshashyn.　Moor special forces families skilled at espionage, sabotage, and assassination, better known to the world as **Assassins** living by the Hashshashyn Code: *By Any Means*.

Shino Bey | Shinobi | Ninja | Forest Demon.　Shino Bey are Families always loyal, doing nothing but obeying their Beys, and Nihon's highest Moor Order, higher than Samoorai, an order to counter Christian Knights. Shino-Bey families are told in the Christian world as Shinobi and in legend as Ninja; yet, there truly is no such thing as Ninja. Shino-Bey did not even wear the Ninja costume made famous through movies. The Ninja costume is a creation of Kobuke Theater. Shino-Bey are Assassin Families living by The Hashshashyn Code: *By Any Means*. The famous Sanomooru and Ninomooru castle guards are Shino-Bey.

Moorkit. Assassin Archer Families living by The Moorkit Code: *By Any Means.* Moorkit are the Moors responsible for the success of the man known in fiction as Dracula.

Shaolin/Tsilin/Tsilum 少林. Warrior/Scholars living by The Code Of Da Moor: *Honor Above All Else Except Loyalty.* Shaolin is a common classification for Kongfu systems associated with The Black Serpent Temple in Kuangdong, China, the first Shaolin Temple overseen by BUDDHA DA MOOR BEY, and The Black Horse Temple in Bey Honan, China, the second Shaolin Temple overseen by BUDDHA DA MOOR BEY.

More on Bey 北

Bey means Bey everywhere in the world and sounds like Bey. In China, Bey is the name of today's northern region, because Beys founded it. Though Bey came to be recognized as the Chinese word for *North*, Bey is older than China itself. Historical and current records hold that Chinese, Mongolian, and Manchurian rulers use Bey 北 as a Family title, political title, and government office, authenticating great warrior spirit and status. For examples, Emperor Liang Bey, **Lin Bey**, **Bey Lin**, and **Lum Bey**.

Beyfu. Older Bey Kongfu systems may use **Bey**, or **Beyfu**, as opposed to **Tsifu** for **Teacher**, in the sense of *obey*, or *the one to obey*. One may use **Beykong** as opposed to **Tsikong** for **Master**; and **Beytaikong**, as opposed to **Tsitaikong** for **Grandmaster**.

Tsi. Tsi is Chinese dialect for Bey. For examples, reference Tsidi, as in **Mao Tsi Tong 1893-1976 Cc**, and the temple political structures of Tsilin, Shaolin, Tsilum, and Wahlum, which is: **Tsitaikong**/Grandmaster, **Tsikong**/Master (who are Graduates and Warrior-Scholars), **Tsifu**/Teacher, **Tsidi**/Disciple, and **Tong Tsi Kong**/Child Studies.

Nan 南. Nan means South, or Serpent, as in the Serpent Temples in Kuangdong [Canton], or southern China. Nan is a **Moorish Latin** [i.e., **Ancient Latin** and Spanish] way of saying that one thing is part of and subordinate to another. Nan Tsilin Temples were subordinate to The Moor Empire, represented by BUDDHA DA MOOR BEY, BUDDHA DAZU HUI KU, Kongfu Bey, and the seven foot dark Moorman, **Emperor Tai Zu**, of The Emperor Fist, also known as Long Fist and Long Arm Kongfu, composed of Black Crane and Blacks Snake Shaolin Kongfu Systems.

Moor Arms and Armor

The study of amour is relevant to Moors and to high-culture. Through such study, one learns that Moors are Europe's indigenous people, in Europe thousands, even millions of years before pale Europeans, as Europe was once connected to Africa, facts, which the Christian-alliance prefers to ignore. All weaponry below was invented by Moors.

Moor Swords.   Moor swords are Crescent Swords, curved like a crescent moon, may be one, or two-handed, made from the best steel, often Damascus steel, and often inscribed with martial, or love poetry. Moor Swords in variation are also known as Shamshir, Mamaluke, Kitara, Katana, Tiger Sword, Sabre, Scimitar, Cutlass, Broadsword, and Rapier.

Moor sheaths are, "richly labored and enameled," carried via baldrics of strong, elaborately decorated leather, according to Washington Irving, author of *Chronicle of the Conquest of Granada* (1894, p. 23).

Ottomahawk   Christian-called, Tomahawk, is a remarkable weapon and hunter tool. An ottomahawk may be ceremoniously given as a peace treaty. Tsalaki tomahawks are traditionally made of silver and encrusted with gems. Those made for peace treaties have built-in pipes, from which cannabis is traditionally smoked to **Make The Peace**.

Moor Armor   Moor armor is traditionally Chainmail or platemail inlaid with gold, silver, and jewels.

Mail   is woven, linked metal that protects body, neck, and face as a tail from the helmet, or as a coif, an example of high culture.

Moor Helmets/Tariks   The Tarik, called so after **Tarik Ben Ziad**, the Moor Emir, to whom Rogers (1952/1980, p. 55) refers, is a round, segmented, spiked, helmet. The spike atop the helmet is like a dagger and made of bronze or iron and gilded with silver or gold. Asians, Romans, Germans, and others adopted Tarik helmets.

Tunic/Hauberk   light type of mail constructed of loops of metal woven to drape to mid-thigh, or knee, split in front and back for horse-riding, sometimes with a hood. Sleeves may be full arm-length, covering hands with leather, or full-mailed gloves. If more protection was desired, a Moor would typically wear a shorter under-layer of armor made of plate, and/or leather.

Moor Shields are large, round sometimes made of anointed elephant or Kamel leather, or Bucklers [small, spiked and metal].

Moor Spears are two and a half-meters long, used offensively of course, but also purely defensively via forming a Tabia, meaning a close formation to serve two functions, one in order to close ranks to provide a safety-wall, and to protect archers.

Compound-Bows fold into three sections for concealment and easy transport, shoots as far as the typical Anglo longbow, yet, is less than half the size and weight.

Moor Hijazi Bows are one or two pieces of wood joined back to back, more compact and more powerful than the Anglo longbow. The Moor Hijazi bow's maximum range for accuracy is 150 meters/164 yards.

Arquebus the first Rifle.

Midfa Hand Canon/First Pistol.

Moor Siege Weaponry/Artillery Archers guard warriors operating siege weaponry, whose heavy engines and baggage were carried on kamelback behind infantry. The Dababah [battering ram]; e.g., is often a multi-level, drivable, wooden siege tower with catapults, all on wheels.

Advanced Weaponry. Moorish weaponry inventions include Submarines and flying devices such as Hang-gliders and Airplanes.

Chapter 3

The Moor People

Who are The Moor People?

Moor People are Earth's original humans, Africans, for common grasps, educators who populated the entire world by all accounts from anthropology, archeology, genetics, biology, and religions, for examples. The Moor Nation, Blood, and Empire is global, truly ancient, and in fact, The Moor Empire is The First World Empire and Order. I elaborate below.

Who are America's Indigenous Moor people? America's Indigenous Moor People are lawfully recognized as Moor Americans, Mooroccan Americans (by any spelling), and Moorish Americans, the largest and most solidly established group, because Moorish Americans are complete with a religion, prophet, and direction for America's Indigenous Moors, especially those whose ancestors were legally enslaved within and by way of the US

Of A, that means between 1776-1865 Cc.

What does Moor Mean?

Moor has three meanings. One meaning by interpretation is, Navigator by the North Pole Star. Moor is synonymous with Navigator, because Moors are the first Navigators of the Seven Seas and the Seven Continents Guided by The North Pole Star. The second meaning, that Moor means More, is a literal translation. **Mohr** is German. **Maur** is French. **Muir/ Muur** is Scottish. And **Moros** is Spanish, as Moors are also Europe's Indigenous Peoples. The third meaning is also a literal translation. Moor means **Love**.

    Moor Languages.   Languages are Moor-created. Nothing else has been proven. That simple. Moors circumnavigated Earth and into several languages, inserted the word, Moor, as the sound of love. For examples, **Amor** is the Spanish and Catalan word for Love, **Amour** is the French word for Love, **Amore** is the Latin and Italian words for Love, and Amar is the Portuguese and Galician word for Love. Thus, all of the above-mentioned languages are Moor languages, languages of Amor, or a Moor, or Love, however one sees.

    The 1887 Cc creators of **Esperanto**, an international auxiliary language designed to foster peace, wisely chose **Mas** as the language's word for love obviously, because in several languages, such as Spanish, Mas means More. Some languages without the Moor sound as their root for Love, have either the EL, or Bey sound. For examples, the Swedish, Norwegian, Danish, and Icelandic word for amor/love is **Elskar. Ljubezen** [Lu-Bey-Sin] is the Slovenian word for love, and **Milestiba** [milestibey] is the Latvian word for love. Bavaria's [originally **Beyern**] modern word for love is **Bev** covering over the original **Bey** sound, as in the Croatian, Macedonian, Serbian, Russian, and Slavic word for love, Lijubav, older-spelled, **Lijubey**. As well the Norwegian word for mother is **Mor**, adding credence to Moorish oral histories of Moorish women raising pale children in love and education.

    Noble Drew Ali instructed that Spanish, also known as Moorish Latin, is the most important language for Moorish Americans to know. Ancient Latin, not today's Church Latin, is the Mother of Amor languages. Never the less, today's Latin, which is mostly Italian, still holds keys to The Moor Empire; for example, the Latin word for Black is Noir, pronounced Nu-wuar, not Moor. It needs to be noted that Hebrew and Arabic are also Imperial Moor languages. The above-mentioned languages are known in Christian public education as **Romance Languages**; yet, there are no Romance languages, because Rome had no language. Furthermore, Rome, also spelled, Rom, is More and Mor backward. Moreover, **The Founder of Rome is Paul Virgo Moor**, also known as **Paulus Virgilus Moros**, known in Christian public education as **Virgil**. Virgil means Virgo. Paulus Virgilus Moros was an astrologer, the norm in Ancient Rome, different than Christian Rome. The Ancient Roman Empire belongs to Moors.

Nevertheless, Rome destroyed The Moor Empire and The Greek Empire, which is a Moor people and government. The only way the world knows anything of Greece; i.e., Greece's language, history, or politics, is because of African and European Moor historians who recorded in Arabic. Yes, there is a Greek language; however, the only way the world knows anything of Ancient Greece is due to Moors writing in Africa and El Andalus. The oldest Greek recorded histories and politics are written in Arabic only.

How does today's Latin hold keys to The Moor Empire? Even today's Latin holds that O is the English language equivalent of I, meaning Personal Self. In Astrology and spiritually, O and I as Self describes a being without beginning, or ending (See the section, Astrology, for the continuance of this line of thought).

Does ish, as in Moorish, diminish the quality of the state of Moor? No, *ish* does not diminish the quality of the state of Moor, because the first usage of ish means, *Of or belonging to a national group.* For examples, British, English, Irish, Polish, Danish, and Jewish. Therefore, definitely, the ish in Moorish is meant respectfully and holds respect. Thus, All Indigenous American Moors and Moorish American Citizens should be proud to identify their Nationality as Moorish American.

In Law, the Moorish American Nationality is respected and powerful and attaches Indigenous Americans as part and parcel to The Moor Empire, The global Moor Nation, The Moorish American Nation, and to Moorocco, as well as to the *1928 Noble Drew Ali-founded American Land Trust*, upon which All Moorish Americans may build. As well Ish is a form of I, as Ich from German. In French, Ish is warlike as in demolish and brandish. Such is from Bey Moors.

Were any Moors/Africans brought from Africa as slaves? According to 1970s Cc Moorish American data, fewer than 10% of American Moors have known ties to one brought from Africa as a slave. Those few who did come from Africa to America as slaves all mixed in and remixed in with

Indigenous Moors over generations. Such mixing has made Indigenous American Moors of approximately all Moors born in America to parents with parent's parents born in America. America is the only homeland that Moorish Americans know and the only origin that one may logically and perhaps lawful claim as one's own.

Of those who came to America from Africa, several came as conquistadors with the Spanish and slavers with the English, Spanish, and French. Then they became enslaved and for the most part, mixed in with indigenous Moors. An example of a group of Moorish African slavers in America, who are not Indigenous Americans are the Jamaican Mooroons. Jamaican Mooroons keep their history preserved in five boroughs: Moor Town, Trelawny, Nanny Town, Scots Town, and Winward.

I being a Black, how do I know if I'm Moor by Blood? Saying, "A Black," in reference to a human should sound odd. In fact, Black, as well as Negro, and Indian, is a socio-political construct to identify a slave, and began in 1779 Cc. However, have you studied enough to know Moors as the indigenous people of America? Yes.

Were you born in America? Yes.

Anywhere in the world, now, or at any time in history, is or has Black ever been a nation with a land, or a flag? No.

Is there a Black God?

Well, kind of. Buddhas, Christs, Tirthankara, for examples, but painted black to show ultimate power; as in The Universe of Black, in which sits all light. However, their national identities, were they Black? No.

Is there a language named Black?

No.

Have you ever seen a slave ship, or even a photo of one, or heard there was a real one some place?

Yes.

What, that one in Georgia that looks like a river barge and un-sea worthy? It may have transported slaves up and down American inner-land waterways, but not intercontinentally. In fact, the only so called evidence of intercontinental slave transport from Africa to America are two rusted shackles found in coastal waters near the Bahama Islands. The only images of slave ships from Africa to America are paintings, recreations, meaning imaginations, and photos of recreations. Yet, there is not one slave ship from Africa to America to be found in any port, museum, or sunk underwater someplace. Technology can find any large structure buried, even in the sea; yet, still, not one slave ship from Africa to America has been recovered. The math on that alone should persuade that so-called Black/African Americans are in fact indigenous to America and by Blood Rights are Moorish American.

Then why should Moorish Americans not just be called American?

American is first described in 1828 *Webster's Dictionary* as, "Copper-people found in the Americas by the Europeans." Copper is dark brown. America breaks down as A Moor I Khan. There is no need for me to dissuade one from this nationality claim. However, because the term, American, is now generalized and no longer recognized as Indigenous, claiming such as an Indigenous nationality creates an extra argument in law. Yet, such is a worthy argument. So for those who want to pursue it, we say, Go for it. The greater focus on nationality proclamations is to get All to proclaim a nationality, any nationality, so that one is recognized as human and not property. Keep in mind that the extra fight on this is steps ahead and that the term, Moorish American, is already established as an Indigenous American nationality, a ball already rolling, a bedrock that has been being built upon for more than 100 years with more room to build upon.

Cherokee and Blackfoot Nations are Moors, so why not just identify as Cherokee, or Blackfoot, for examples? The fes-wearing and turban-wearing Cherokee and Blackfoot Nations are sub-nations under the Moor Nation, all within the Moor Empire. Moor is the parent and grand-nation. All other nations are sub-nations. Sometimes within sub-nations are sub-nations. For example, Cherokee, which is actually Tsalaki (Ts Allah Ki) has seven-sub nations and one of those sub-nations, Bird, has three sub-nations, clans, or tribes: Eagle, Raven, and Turtle Dove; yet, all have rightful claims and should also claim Moor in their descent and allegiance.

American is now defined to include anyone born in America. Does that make all Americans Moors? No. However, foreigners may, through naturalization, become Moorish American Citizens, equal to Moor National Citizens. However, status is still recognized by Nation, or lack of. Thus, a Moorish American Citizen may be of any Nation just like a US citizen, or citizen of Mexico, Moorocco, or China, for examples.

How Are Moors Ancient? Moors trace to the most ancient of all times to **The Olmecs** in **México**, which originally included Guatemala, Beliz, El Salvador, Honduras, Nicaragua, and Costa Rica, with pyramids and other great stone works, and to **The Somoors** Of **Somooria** through *Cuniform Tablets* and other great stone works where Moors are found as **High Priests of Anno** (Christian-written as Anu) and trace to the city, **Taadmoor.**

Moorish Americans are the first in America, the Pyramid/Mound-Builders, creators of America's Great Seal. Approximately 90% of American Moors recall an ancestor being Cherokee, Blackfoot, or Washitaw, for examples, instead of being a slave from Africa across the Atlantic Ocean. The fewer than about 10% who do, also recall blood-ties to Lakota, Seminole, or Creek, for more examples, all turban and fez-wearing Moors. Yet, these are not the oldest nations. Thus, Moorish American ties to America's Most Ancient People. Our claim is **Autokthonus**, meaning, "From Earth." We do not claim to be have walked to America on some unproven land called The Baring Strait, to have come from monkeys, or outer-space, as all detach one from Land Rights.

Moors by different Identities

Moros Moors of México, Central America, South America, and the Mooralika Islands, what the Christians call the Philippines after King Phillip II of Spain, for examples.

Mooroccans Moors of Moorocco. America is Moorocco, in fact, referenced as Maghreb El Agsa, the Farthest West portion of Moorocco. The continents were once connected.

Moorons those of a Royal Mongolian Family.

In Christian Classics, Moor is a term correct for any dark-skinned person. Christian education systems explain away Ancient America as the time before pale Europeans came to America by saying that they do not know what was before them and refer to the time before them as Pre-

Columbian. Such is fine, because every people have their story. And the Moor Story is simple, that we know what was before. It was The Moor Pyramid government system of Ali, EL, Bey and we are still here. México is mostly Moors. Parts of Canada all the way to Panama used to be México and the people are mostly Moors. Cuba, Dominican Republic, Guyana, Columbia, and others are all populated mostly by Indigenous Moors.

Borinken Moors. Indigenes of what is now called Puerto Rico, a socio-political stamp, or construction, not a Nation. Identity with **Bordiquo/a** is identity with Borinken Moors. Borinken mixed with pale Europeans and formed the Moorish Taíno Tribe.

Taíno Moors. A newer Moor Nation formed from Borinken Moors and pale Europeans.

Arawak Moors. Indigenes of what is called Dominican Republic.

Mexican derives from *Amexem*, Mex means Mix, as in mixing bloods. Therefore, there are Mixtec, Mextec, and Aztec. México is also home to Moros, Morenas, Mooroons, Ráramori, and several other peoples with the Moor sound in name and land, as well as in their faces, hair, musics, foods, drinks, and terms of endearment.

Arab. Moors are the first Arabs, according to J. A. Rogers, 1952/1980, p. 13, 25), first to use the Arabic language, and described by Arab writers of all times as *dark, Kush*, and of *the purest Arabian blood*.

Black as a people identifier, is a slave-stamp used by Europeans to replace the term, Moor. Black is an adjective, meaning something that describes, but is not a noun. People are nouns, and cannot be adjectives. Into the 1950s Cc, black was a fighting word on the same level with nigger. *Webster's New Twentieth Century Dictionary of English Language Unabridged* (Whitehall, 1956) relates that a Moor is (a) "A native of the northern coast of Africa, called by the Romans from the color of the people, Mauritania, the country of dark complexioned people; a native of Morocco," (b) "a member of any of the African or Asian dark races," and (c) "a black." And according to the Oxford English Dictionary (2004), Moors are, "people commonly black," a description that Christian media promotes as a people. Yet, *black/blec* is a slave stamp and economic status meaning *colorless*. Black was first applied to pale Europeans, especially those who enslaved themselves in order to come to America. Black means one owes.

Never the less, several people have codified messages in attempt to identify Moor with black; e.g., Cleveland has an entire project community named Morris Black, with the message that Moor is Black and Moorish is Black.

Blackamoor. Proof Moor does not mean Black and that Black was used to replace Moor. Otherwise this would say, Black-a-Black.

American Indian. **How about American Indian for a nationality?** First, let us discuss India.

India. India is a land with citizens of several different nationalities surrounded by the Indian Ocean and the Arabian Sea, separate from America, which is surrounded by the Atlantic and Pacific Oceans. Most of what Americans think of as India is actually Hindustan, land and people. India is merely a state within Hindustan. A portion of Indians converted to Islam, broke from Hindustan and became Pakistan. Alas, Indian is not an American Nationality. The construct, American Indian, is a misnomer, a mistake. As a national descriptor, American Indian is as vague and ineffective as African American, as both mention two continents; yet, no Nation. Thus, in USA law, one who claims Indian as an American Nationality claims a misnomer and becomes stateless and categorized as Negro (see below).

Negro. In law, Negro means Dead, a fiction with a fictional history, and not human. Negro began c. 1600 Cc as a slave-stamp placed on pale Europeans by Moors. Negro relates to a primate ancestor of pale peoples. Europeans turned the negro slave-stamp backwards on Moors to replace the term, Moor, like Rome turned More backwards. In *Webster's New Twentieth Century Dictionary of English Language Unabridged* (1956), Whitehall relates that a Moor is, "a negro," and African literature identifies *Indigenous Moors as Advanced* and *Backward Moors as Negroes*. S. Johnson, author of *A Dictionary of the English Language in two volumes* (1776), agrees.

Indian. Indian is another European-used slave-stamp to replace the term, Moor from 1776 to 1865 Cc by force, and now willingly by usurpers taking advantage of government programs, pretenders, Five-Dollar Indians, and the unsuspecting. However, Indian means **Without GOD**. In US Law, Indian and Negro are the same. Indian is not the same as **Indios** from the Spanish language meaning, **With GOD**.

26

Autokthon means, **From Earth**. The Moorish American claim to origins is an autokthonous claim. We do not claim to be from another planet, Gods, angels, extra-terrestrials, or monkeys, all of which would nullify the Moorish American Indigenous Heir Apparent Claim to America as the Moor's Ancestral Estate with entitled Birthrights, described as Rights to Self, Land, Water, Air, Allodial, Unalienable, Inalienable, Primogeniture, Inheritance, Noble, Substantive, Freehold, and Descendable. However, Autokthon, or the state of being autokthonous is not a nationality.

Asiatic. In Moorish American legend, *Asiatic means **Human.*** The legend says that all of Earth was once called Asia. However, Asiatic has never been a Nation. Though Asiatic is United States Race Code (USRC) 463, Asiatic is a derogatory label for Asians and a hindsight term that generalizes history and describes no one. Proving Asiatic is not required for Moorish American Nationality and can only complicate the argument.

US RACE CODES

The US government allows people to disenfranchise themselves by identifying with the wrong US Race Code (*https://www.cdc.gov/nchs/data/dvs/RaceCodeList.pdf*), or mistaken identity. Among US Race Codes, three, Moor 667, American 995, and Moroccan 633, are acceptable for Moorish Nationality. Several choices are ridiculous and laughable, yet, codified non-human, non-nationality choices offered by the US, which disenfranchises Indigenous Peoples. Below, I reordered some US Race Codes to show relevance to one another. All are real and not jokes:

201 Black	604 Central American
203 African American	606 Chilean
204 AfroAmerican	605 Chicano
634 North African	610 Ecuadorian
205 Nigritian	613 Hispanic
206 Negro	615 Latin American
207 Bahamian	616 Mestizo
208 Barbadian	618 Nicaraguan
220 Other African	619 Panamanian
299 Multiple BLACK or	621 Peruvian
AFRICAN AMERICAN	629 Venezuelan
responses	632 Cayman Islander
468 Yello	622 Puerto Rican

623	Morena	673	Rainbow
624	South American	674	Octoroon
626	Spanish American	675	Quadroon
631	Tejano	676	Multiracial
640	Dominican Republic	677	Interracial
641	Dominican Islander	678	Multiethnic
643	Bermudan	679	Multinational
644	Aruba Islander	681	CANADIAN
646	Guyanese	683	IBERIAN
		684	TRIGUENO
652	Brown	990	Multiple SOME OTHER RACE responses
653	Bushwacker		
656	Chocolate	699	OTHER RACE, N.E.C. 14
658	Coffee	996	Uncodable
659	Cosmopolitan	997	Deferred
660	Issues	998	Unknown
662	Melungeon	999	First Pass Reject
663	Mixed	A95	Central American Indian
666	Mulatto	A97	Mexican American Indian
668	Biracial	A98	south AMerican Indian
672	Half Breed	A99	Spanish American Indian

Note: White is the first US Race Code, Code 101.

America

America is **Amoorika**, and **Amoorocco**, being that since The European Dark Ages, vowels have been interchangeable. [The Book Of Moors explains in depth and provides ample examples]. As well Amooroka is **Moorocco, Maghrib El Aqsa/المغرب الأقصى/The Farthest West**, And **Seat Of The Moor Empire, North Africa**, and **The Temple Of the Moon And Star ☾**. North America is Northwest Africa, **Turtle Island** and **The North Gate** (of the world). **South America is The South Gate**. In the US Marine Anthem, The Moor Empire, "Enemies," are listed as stretching, "from The Halls Of Montezuma [Moortekzoma in México] to the Shores Of Tripoli [in Africa]."

The Moorish American National Flag is The Moor Empire Flag, the red one with the centered, green, inter-locking, five-sided star, The Imperial Moor Star, which is three dimensional and contains 96 triangles found with mathematics no higher than algebra, more with calculus and non-Euclidean geometry. (Note that the legs on The Mooroccan Kingdom Flag are flat and do not interlock). The green of The Imperial Star represents peace. The red of The Imperial Flag represents Moor blood. The Imperial Star's five sides for the past about 200 years, represents Love, Truth, Peace, Freedom, and Justice. However, the ancient and continuing representations of The Imperial Star's five sides are Fire, Earth, Air, Water, and Spirit, which comes from Astrology and is the same in Buddhism, and Kongfu.

The Moor Imperial Flag is a symbol of male rule without female interference as evidenced by the absence of the Imperial Crescent Moon Symbol. In older times, The Imperial Flag was solid red, without symbols, and called The Blood Flag to reflect bloodshed, the symbol of Moor versus Moor wars.

The Great Seal Of America is The Pyramid.

Moors' National Monuments are Pyramids.

Moors' Ancestral Titles are linked to the three branches of Moor government, Executive, Legislative, and Enforcement.

Ali   is the executive branch of Moor government and means, Master.

EL   is the legislative branch of Moor government and means, Eternal Light.

Bey   is the enforcement branch of Moor government and means, Those to Obey.

EL and Bey are older than the Moabite GODs, EL, BEY, and BAAL, and may originate with the Canaanite GODS, BEY and EL, Christian-written as BA'AL and BAAL. Moorish Americans hold that the Ali title is reserved for Royals. No Moorish American is supposed to be so bold as to declare oneself an Ali. Noble Drew Ali instructed that each Moor should carry just one title, EL or Bey. Thus, each Moorish American National should carry either the title, EL, or Bey, and each Moorish American Natural should carry the title, Ibn EL, or Ibn Bey.

Dey   is a Moor title of Africa and Europe, and approximately 200 years old. Those who claim this title disenfranchise themselves from Indigenous American Status.

AL   is a Moor title of South America and Europe. Those who claim this title must be careful not to disenfranchise themselves from Indigenous American Status. For example, one born in North America claiming Al.

Moorish American Religion and Religious Issues

American religious stability is founded on Noble Drew Ali as an American Prophet, which enables religious freedoms and protections. "If the Prophet is not Right, the Temple is not Right," is a Moorish American Holy Mantra for religious power.

What is the Moorish American Religion?   More important than differences in religions and religious descriptors is the ability for Moorish Americans to consolidate strength of numbers in one united religious descriptor. ISLAM is a uniting religious descriptor for Moors, Moorish Americans, and for Moor Americans and the only one needed on official paperwork and without explanation. Below, for academic's sake, not for faction identification, let us examine ISLAM from various eyes.

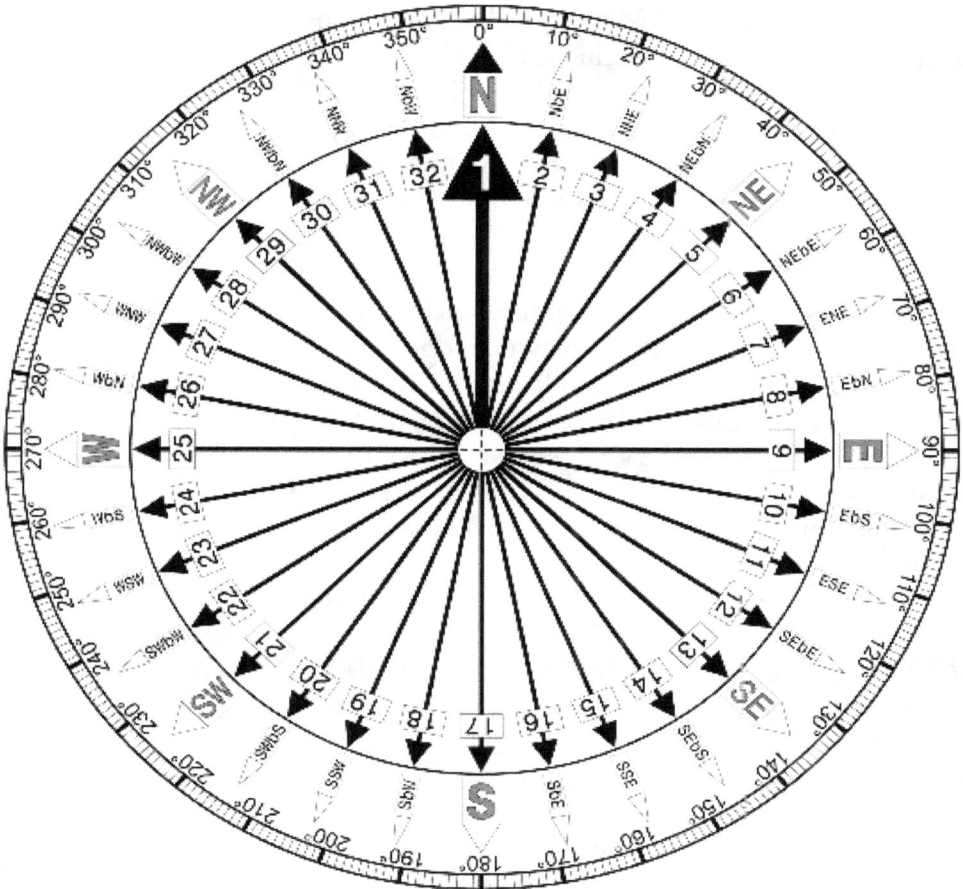

Fig. 3   A Compass Card showing the math of 32 spaces that make up 360° and makes navigating easier.

Islam.   As an Arabic word, Islam means The Peace. Several different religious factions, some of them in opposition to one another, claim the religion, Islam. Identifying a particular faction to which one belongs is not only unnecessary, such is advised against, because such targets one as an enemy to several others. All are without Indigenous Moorish American attachment.

Islamism.   Even adherents to Islamism may simply use ISLAM as a religious descriptor for unity and with honor. Never the less, Islamism must be described as Noble Drew Ali describes, because He invented such. On necessary paperwork, Islamism may be described as, "The Indigenous Religion of Moorish Americans, whose symbols include The Imperial Crescent Moon And Star."

O, Old Order ISLAM.   From The Moor Empire, The Moors' *Ancient Religion* is **O**, meaning Old Order ISLAM, and The Self Law Of I. To begin explaining, O, as already learned, is the Latin language character for I, meaning Self. Therefore, The Self Law Of I and The Self Law of O are the same. Old Order ISLAM is a navigation tool by way of Zodiak Astrology that describes ALLAH as ALL LAW, Universal Law, and The Self Law of I as the same. O is also the ancient hieroglyph for Completion, 360°, a Zodiac Wheel, and Immortality.

Thinking of one's self as complete enables mental, social, spiritual, and martial strength. Such is known among adepts of The Moorish Science Temple Of America, followers of Buddha, Kongfu (Confucius to Christians), Jesus, and Mohammed. All are united by the Imperial Moor Astrological Symbol, The Crescent Moon And Sun. According to Noble Drew Ali (*The Holy Koran*, p.7, III. 14), as taught by Charles Mosley Bey on a mission in Cleveland, Ohio, ISLAM is an acronym meaning I Self Law Am Master.

The Self Law of I is from Ancient Moor Masters who studied people as creators and inspired The Moor Empire Motto and direction, *MAN, KNOW THYSELF AND THOU WILL KNOW THE UNIVERSE AND THE GODS*. Such is conventionally known in part by the Greek aphorism, *KNOW THYSELF*, words Moorish-educated Socrates supposedly repeated through the writings of his pupil, Plato, and the writings of Plato's pupil, Aristotle, teacher of Alexander the Great, who held the Greek Empire together for all of its approximately three and a half years. Kongfu and the Buddha and Founder of Shaolin Temple, Da Moor Bey, taught that **The Golden Rule Of Kongfu** is **O**, or **I**, depending on how one sees self.

ISLAM, The Self Law Of I, is a command to Know Thyself. It needs to be said that I is a straight line that came from nowhere and is going nowhere, which also suggests infinity. We learn this from Euclidean geometry from the Greek man, Euclid, c. 300 BCc. Yet, by that analogy, I is a two-dimensional argument for comprehension of self and useless for us three-dimensional humans who need the O and 360° in order to comprehend self with sight. Culturally and traditionally, Moors are to always study. Religiously, Moors are aways to study self, the only way to live within one's own mind and not the mind of another. ISLAM and Kongfu are based on Astrology.

Astrology.   Astrology is a Latin word that in English means **Math**. **Astrologer** is a Latin word that in English means **Mathematician**. The suffix *ology* means *the study of*. *Astro* means *the Heavens*. Thus, Astrology literally translates to, The Study of the Heavens, and Astrology is The Study of Heaven's effects on Humans on Earth.

Math is the Language of The Universe. Astrology, Math, Old Order ISLAM, The Self Law Of I, is The One Universal Truth. Such is Moorish Science, the subject of the sacred mission, for which Noble Drew Ali sent Charles Mosley Bey to Cleveland, Ohio.

Since the beginning of recorded history, learned people world-wide have felt that Astrology is the primary, functional, and traditional tool for navigation not just of self, but also through, for examples, land, water, air, space, and relationships, both social and business. Astrology is the one universal science that effects all and connects each human to one another and to the Heavens. Governments, military, and the wealthy use Astrology to navigate life decisions, and each child born is affected by Astrology. Financier, JP Morgan, one of the world's richest men ever, said, "Anyone can be a millionaire, but to become a billionaire you need an astrologer."

Astrological knowledge is holdable power and an invaluable skill. For examples, Astrology tells when to plant and when to pluck foods in order to extract maximum nutrients. Astrology shows our strengths and weaknesses in the past, present, and future. Astrology is medicinal and therapeutic, because Astrology is the one way to know self. Astrology is the science that Freemasons practice in ritual with astrological tools such as the compass, square, and level. Astrology through the Moon guides ocean tides and women's wombs. One's own raw energy can do wonders; yet, Astrology is helpful to success in all endeavors.

There are 10 Zodiak Planets and 12 Zodiak Constellations that move through the 12 Houses all day and night, every day and every night. We chart 10 planets, Our Sun, Our Moon, Mars, Mercury, Venus, Jupiter, Saturn, Uranus, Neptune, and Pluto, yet, not Earth. Earth is our Ground-Zero, where we are in the map of Our Solar System.

A Birthchart is laid on a Zodiak Wheel in order for one to know self, which largely means being able to mathematically see one's strengths and weaknesses for the purpose of focus, improvement, and command. A birthchart is a treasure-map to universal power, GOD-given power, if one perceives as such.

BUDDHA DA MOOR BEY.   Prophet Noble Drew Ali instructed Moorish Americans to follow the teachings of BUDDHA. Yet, there are several. MAI curriculum teaches of two BUDDHAS. The First is BUDDHA PRINCE SIDHARTHA GUATAMA BEY. He was born in a political geographical area called a Shaka. The second is BUDDHA DA MOOR BEY, the Founder of Shaolin Kongfu, Shaolin Temple, Shaolin Buddhism, Cha'an Buddhism, and Zen Buddhism, the Way of Samoorai.

BUDDHA PRINCE SIDHARTHA said, "Cause no harm to the living." The BUDDHA DA MOOR BEY, a warrior commissioned to transform Buddhists into warriors, added to Buddhism, "One may harm the living, if harm is threatened." Thus, began Da Moor Buddhism, which is Shaolin Buddhism, also known as Cha'an Buddhism and Zen Buddhism. On the highest levels, Shaolin Kongfu teaches to attack body parts according to Astrology.

Numerology.   Numerology is the study of numbers, therefore, Numerology also deals with math/Astrology, and is a Moorish Science. Astrology converts meaningful numbers into shapes such as squares, triangles, circles, and sextiles, for examples.

The Number 7.   Shapes and being affected by their sight are part of human genetic codes and convey astrological messages even to pre-crawling babes. Perhaps the most meaningful shape/symbol to be studied first is the number 7. However, we need to see the number 7 in original form, Moor form (See Figure 1 to the right). Count the angles, or bends in the lines and one counts seven angles, or seven bends.

Fig. 1 A number 7 in its original Moor form.

Astrology/Math is represented by The-Crescent-Moon-And-Star Symbol, which has five points on the Star and two on the Crescent, for a total of seven points. So why is 7 so important? 7 represents Universal Balance, GOD. 7 is G, the seventh letter of the Anglo alphabet centered in the masonic compass and square symbol. 7 is the pyramid shadow within the circle on The Great Seal Of America as seen on the reverse side of the US one-dollar bill. **7** represents **ALL LAW**, meaning, **ALLAH**, The Universe, Universal Law, Universal Balance, Libra, The Seven Days of Creation, The Seven Continents, The Seven Oceans, The Seven Classical Planets (Sun, Moon, Mercury, Mars, Venus, Jupiter, and Saturn), the perfect pH balance, and the Seven Main Human Body Systems (Circulatory, Digestive, Endocrine, Immune, Musculo-Skeletal, Nervous, and Respiratory). We need balance in all things. How do we balance? Tools known as compass, square, level, plumb, pencil, and others help.

Balance self to off-balance others   (Kongfu).

The Circle 7 Symbol.   On the book commonly referred to as <u>The Circle 7 Koran</u>, the circle around the pyramid is not actually a circle, because it has breaks representing Earth's North, East, South, and West Gates, which are The Vernal Equinox at Aries, Summer Solstice At Cancer, Autumnal Equinox at Libra, and Winter Solstice at Capricorn. Each are Moor Holidays, which happen regardless of belief. Each of four lines represent three Zodiak Signs.

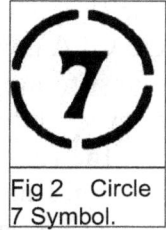

Fig 2   Circle 7 Symbol.

Moorish American Governments

Sultanate.   A Sultanate is a traditional Moor government ruled by a **Sultan**, or a **Sultana**. Sultan and Sultana means **Authority**. A Sultan, or Sultana is the ultimate ruler concerning all Sultanate matters, as kingdoms are overseen by kings, counties by counts, and duchies by a duke, or a duchess. The Hebrew word for Sultan is **Shilton**. Both words, Sultan and Shilton, derive from the word **Salata**, from both Arabic and Hebrew, and means **To be Strong**.

Sultans rule through inheritance, or appointment by The Emperor. Today, without an Emperor, bodies of Moors may appoint a Sultan, or one may act as Sultan so that Moors may have local governments and communal bases.

Traditionally, Sultanate law systems are governed by **Millet, Sharia, Imperial Decree, Royal Decree,** and/or **legislative powers** granted by Royal Decree, or mixtures. Modern Sultanate law systems may also be mixed with Anglo-Saxon laws; for example, the Sultanate of Oman. Under Sultanates are republiks, all under The Emperor and The Moor Empire, as are kingdoms, counties, and duchies, for examples.

A Sultan is different than a **Malik**, or a King in that the Sultan title carries religious significance; yet, without claiming **The Khalifate**, or ultimate Imperial Rule. A Malik, or a King is traditionally a ruler without religious significance. However, England, for example, controlling land and the Anglo Church is an exception. In 1957 Cc, in Christian partnership with France, Moorocco changed from a Sultanate to a Kingdom.

Republik.   A Republik is a Moor, Moorish, and Mooroccan form of government created by and subordinate to a Sultanate. For example, the US Of A Republik was created and sanctioned by and subordinate to The Moor Empire under Sultan Mohammed Tsidi 3rd Bey. In republiks The People hold government power, through elected representatives. The US Of A government is a republik, not a democracy. <u>Article IV of the Constitution for the US Of A</u> recognizes a Republik form of Government to every state in the US Of A.

The Republik Color is red, like The Moor Empire and like in US politics. Think Republicans Red and Democrats Blue. During US Of A and US slavery times, Republicans, Reds, were anti-slavery. Whereas Democrats, Blues, were pro-slavery.

Moorish American Greetings

As Salaamu Alaiykum and Wa Alaiykum Salaam.   As Salaamu Alaiykum and Wa Alaiykum Salaam are globally-recognized as honorable and respectful greetings and departures. One arriving, or departing may initiate such exchange. As Salaamu Alaiykum, the greeting, means, May peace be upon you all, with, "you all," culturally meaning, You and your family, and religiously meaning, You and your guardian angels. Wa is the Arabic sound for, And, therefore, Wa Alaiykum Salaam, the cultural reply, means, May the peace be upon you all (also). However, Moorish Americans tend to greet each other in the Moorish American way.

ISLAM and Peace.   Moorish Americans have developed a culture of greeting with the acronym, ISLAM, meaning I Self Law Am Master, a constant reminder of The Self Law Of I and spiritual connection to Math, the Universe, and to ALL LAW. Moorish Americas depart with the word, Peace. It must be noted that, Islam, is an Arabic word meaning, The Peace; whereas, Salaam means Peace and Islam, the Arabic word, may be written with Latin characters as, Isalaam.

MAI, The Moorish Circle Of Mothers and Sons, and Other Moor Groups.   Like other Moor organizations, MAI and The Moorish Circle Of Mothers and Sons enjoy a special greeting.

Gripping Hands.   Moorish Americans grip and press toward one another, but do not shake and will release the grip if shaking is insisted.

Imperial Moor Salute is presented with feet on a 45° angle, the right hand placed over the heart, elbow out sideways, left palm held high with elbow bent on a 90° angle so that the body makes seven right angels just like the true number, 7.

Imperial Moor Warrior Salute/The Crescent And Son Salute

Moor warriors of old, Kongfu practitioners, and others traditionally present this salute with right hand lain over top of the left fist, representing the Crescent Moon And Son, as well as the Yin/Yang Symbol, and Turban/Turbine Energy Symbol.

Bowing. Bowing is not a Moorish custom, or culture in salutation, or religion. Moors do not bow. A Moor's head is to remain up and noble with eyes wide open to receive light. In Moorish American religion, Sheiks do not ask that one spend time with head down and eyes closed imagining the unseen.

Moorish Activities

Fencing. Fencing, invented by Moors, is sword-play between friends, and has three different swords with different rules such as striking zones, for example. In America, there are not enough fencers to take advantage of all of the college funds for fencers. In order to receive funds, a fencer does not need to win, or to be particularly good at all. One is only required to make practices and to do one's best in competition, which is why MAI promotes Fencing.

Chess. Chess, invented by Moors, is a war-game incorporating math, planning, strategizing, and imagining towards goals. On higher skill-levels, chess is an art. Chess seems to represent the struggle between Moors and Christians by virtue of the color of the pieces alone. Another attestation to such idea are the facts of the roles of the pieces being changed from Moorish rules to Christian rules.

Moorish nobles mixed with European commoners so much that all European nobility became blood-related. Therefore, in order to protect nobles, special war rules, such as capture, not kill, was put in place. In the game of chess, such is represented by the treatment of the king versus all of the other pieces. Nobles may play games with peasant lives; yet, not even knights, or holy men may harm a noble. Chess may be a simple game now, perhaps. Yet, Chess is a noble and legal device that settled battles, even entire wars, and drew landlines without bloodshed, because by Moorish tradition, "The Most Intelligent Should Rule."

US public education systems relate that the origins of chess are lost and that the oldest Christian chess writing is from the 16th century Cc, authored by Ruy Lopez. However, chess dates at least as far back as 1146 Cc as evidenced by The Royal Moor Flag Of House EL Moorhad (Mohade) of Moorocco, which features the chessboard centered, which replaced The Imperial Crescent Moon And Star Symbol.

The Moor *Elephant* pieces, Christians turned into bishops and the Moor *War Minister,* Christians turned into a queen, according to Bill Price, author of *The History of Chess in Fifty Moves* (2015, p. 39), and turned the horse pieces into knights. In Moor chess rules, black moves first, representing **The Black Battle Flag**, an honorable announcement of war-intentions and a representation of death.

Middle Era Chess is a term I use to describe when chess was played with a queen as opposed to the war minister; yet, black still moved first, the king entered battle to protect his queen, and the goal was to mate the queen, not the king.

Chess's Three Phases.   Chess's three phases are the Beginning, Middle, and End.

Lesson #1: The End Game – To Attack, Defend, or Counter and Which Pieces Are Better, When and Why?

Lesson #2: The Beginning Game – Fighting for squares, Preparing a Break, and Creating Weaknesses in the Enemy's Structure.

Lesson #3: The Middle Game – Identifying the Weakest Point, Developing a Plan of Attack, Combinations, and Choosing Which Pieces to Trade.

Chess lessons may be applied to real life. The most important chess lesson for real life is goal-setting. Beginning with a thought, a goal is set, and energy is put into motion. Next, one learns to hone concentration, patience, and diligence in order to get closer and closer to one's goal. In art and in life, goals may be molded, manipulated, and altered.

We must calculate the logic of a goal, or a decision using math. In chess, one spends time deciding which pieces are worth the most and on what squares each would be best placed. Likewise, in life one does well to make such decisions with social and business relations, for examples.

One who plays chess, comes to have friends who play chess. As one's skills improve so may one's circles of friends. Juniors tend to hang with juniors. Experts and masters tend to hang with experts and masters, who typically are people who also have other skills.

For those who do not yet know how to play chess, I suggest learning. One is never too old to gain a skill, have fun, and earn respect from people from all walks of life, regardless of language, or socio-economic barriers.

Red Circle.   A Red Circle is a War Band. Warriors from any of Families, or Clans may join a Red Circle. Red Circle members wear red turbans and red sashes.

Social Eating.   Moors eat with the right hand and never reach in communal food with the left hand. Moors put soiled napkins on the floor to be collected later, as opposed to on a table, or next to food, so as not to contaminate.

Debts.   A Moor never forgets a debt, no matter how much time has passed, and is obligated to repay.

Making Friends.   When a Moor makes friends, the friendship is for life.

Bathing.   Bathing and overall cleanliness is a fundamental and a large part of Moorish culture throughout the world. Moors even named places in Europe, Bath, as places where others could come and learn how to bathe.

Bathhouses.   Bathhouses are a Moorish invention. Under Moorish government, it is appalling to all for one to present one's self socially while reeking with foul odors. Being funky is rude and disrespectful, especially when bathhouses were abundant. Bathhouses are not traditionally just for cleansing, but also places of social congregation. Traditionally in bathhouses, people drink wine, smoke cannabis, read poetry, and socialize in other ways such as helping a friend, or a few wash hands, backs, or more, for examples.

Washing Hands.   If two people can put their hands in dirt together, they can put their hands in soap and water together. Nothing else makes sense. Thus, a Moorish tradition of friendship is Washing Hands. Two people, or more simply soap and wash each other's hands. Washing Hands is a clean practice that should continue with clean thoughts. Therefore, the following poem is inspired by the mood of clean thoughts and bathhouses.

Think Mink

Our words at will may splurge like mink
carefully wording to recall tales in ink
a listening elixir, a drunk's ear-drink

They call us clever and never say we stink
I love Moor people and all that we think,
Some dark temples are lit with the pink

At Moor social washings in golden sinks
Rub me, scrub me, wash what you think
in jeweled tubs, soaping friends with mink.

Moorish Items

Turban.   A turban is a symbol of Moor Nobility, Birthright, and Turbine Power, worn by men, women, and children on the head and/or around the shoulders, or waist as a **Rumel, Sash, Sarong, cloak,** or **cape** with, or without a decorative jewel as a clasp. The turban may be used to bathe, warm, rock in a hammock, or as a sling to carry objects.

In warfare the turban may be used in order to attack, defend, dress a wound, or sling a limb. Some Turban-ways of the Hashshashyn, known as Assassins, are globally-known. Turbans represent **Turbine Power**, meaning everything with a fan, for examples, windmills, watermills, airplanes, cars, refrigerators, and computers.

Cloak, Cape, Burnoose, Qob   are outer-wear worn primarily to keep indoor clothing clean and protected from outdoor elements.

Fes   The fes has been worn by royal and noblemen since ancient times. Such is seen in several nation's relics and artwork as symbols of birthright, the womb, and Earth, from where Moors originate. The Red Fes, red like The Moorish American Flag, is the fes of the Moors.

The fes's knot atop the tassel represents a nipple. The Moorish fes's tassel is free to rotate the full-circle, representing 360° of knowledge. The masonic and Shriner feses are fixed to within 32°, representing the 32 spaces that make up 360° on a compass, as seen on what is called a compass card, an astrological navigation tool as seen in Figure 3, p 37.

Tassel on the right side, or tassel on the left side?   In Moor tradition, the initiate wears tassel hanging left. The graduate wears tassels hanging right, symbolizing a move toward the positive. For Christians, the reverse is true, for example, the Shriner tassel is fixed on the left side

Black Fes.   The Black Fes represents and is reserved for one learned in martial arts and law. Mofti/Mufti wear black feses. Is there a difference between Mofti and Mufti? Perhaps just symbolically. Mofti has a complete circle, whereas, U is seen as a cut-off, a beheading, missing information.

Fes, Turban, and Tassel Adornments.   Moorish Americans traditionally do not mark there feses, because an unmarked fes shows that one is free, according to Noble Drew Ali. Men sometimes sport the fes with a turban wrapped around. Sometimes the turban may sport a jewel. This makes for ease off and on. Tassels and turbans may sport plumes/

feathers of various birds relating to one's nation, or sub-nation.

Plumes/Feathers/Writing pens. Plumes worn in tassels and turbans represent a Warrior/Scholar, scribe, and authority, and that the pen is mightier than the sword. A war chief, for example, a Tsalaki war chief, wears a bonnet of plumes, with which he may write a thousand war declarations. (Cherokee is the Christian word for Tsalaki).

Moors value certain plumes as powerful Earth and Spirit Symbols. A single plume may cost hundreds of dollars. The traditional way to acquire a spirit plume is to find it, not kill the bird and take the feathers. The bird must leave the plume. One sacred bird of the Tsalaki, for example, is the Tsalaki Owl, also known as the Spirit Owl, High Magic Owl, Screech Owl, and Hoot Owl, Horned Owl to Christians. Other sacred Tsalaki birds are the Egret and Heron. The greatest and most favored plumes of all come from the Great Blue Heron.

A Christian belief is that owls are possessed creatures and their cry is an evil omen called a *Bray*.

Hakama Pants. Hakama pants are baggy and short at, or tight on about mid-calf down, and a crotch that may bag as low as to the knees.

Tunic is blousy shirt for fashion, or tighter chainmail armor worn for protection, covers to mid thigh, or just above, or below the knees.

Poet Shirts are blousy, v-neck, ruffle-sleeved shirts worn for fashion.

Kaftan is a woman's long and long-sleeved fashionable dress.

Peace Pipes often double as Ottomahawks and when one does, it asks the question, "Peace or death?" Tobacco and peyote are smoked in peace pipes; yet, more commonly, Cannabis, which is Indigenous.

Wampum/Bandolier/Banda is a traditional pocketed band to hold a warrior's needs, worn slung from right shoulder to left side of the waist. Banda is the model for the Christian rosary.

Unnecessary Claims in Pursuit of Moorish American Nationality.

Claiming Asiatic, Moabite, Canaanite, Israelite, Hebrew, Jew, Nubian, Nuwaubian, Dugdahmoundyah, Egyptian, Olmec, and/or Extra-terrestrial as identity is an unnecessary challenge in describing Moorish American Nationality, as well claiming such may defeat the Moorish American Indigenous argument. There is no record of a time when Earth was called Asia. Thus, at best, we settle for accepting the term, Asiatic, as related to a nation of people as Moorish mythology and oral tradition. Noble Drew Ali instructed to use one's own mind to save one's self. Some Moorish Science Temple literature, with which I disagree, goes so far as to encourage Moors to identify as, "Afro-Asiatic," offering the following explanations:

> The languages of the Afroasiatic family, divided into six branches, Egyptian, Semitic, Berber, Cushitic, Omotic, and Chadic, which some think to have first been spoken along the shores of the Red Sea, Africa.

The problem with such is no such people ever referred to themselves as Afro-Asiatic, or Asiatic. In fact, such terms were created in hindsight by Europeans belonging to Christian institutions. As well choosing more than one heritage, or race response on Censuses, for example, results in one not being recognized with any Nation and gets one boxed into one of the following categories, Multiple SOME OTHER RACE responses Code 990, Uncodable Code 996, Deferred Code 997, UNKNOWN Code 998, First Pass Reject Code 999, Multiple Black or African American responses Code 299, or Multiple ASIAN responses Code 499.

Is there any evidence of anyone in the past or present who spoke, or who speaks a language called Asiatic now?

No.

Does anyone now, or has anyone ever spoken Afro-Asiatic?

No. In all my years in countries and schools, I have never ran across even mention of an Asiatic, or an Afro-Asiatic language, so I logically conclude that such is because there are no Asiatics and never were. Such problems are why Moorish Science Temples Of America, for examples, do not issue Nationality documents, or Nationality identification cards. The

Moorish American Nation conflicts with The Asiatic Nation. One is of Moors. The other is a derogatory term for Asian and an imagined Nation.

Why not use Moroccan, or Moroccan American as a Nationality, since Moorish Americans have also been described as "Moroccans born in America?"

Some have a functional path to link to The Moor Empire. However, a Moroccan American is a National of the Kingdom Of Morocco, Africa, which is perfectly fine, yet, not for Indigenous American Moors.

May non-Moslems Claim Moorish American Nationality?

Yes, because only Ancestral Religion, not personal religion, is a Nationality subject. Ancestral Religion must be acknowledged, because acknowledging ancestral religion is one of five parts required in Law for Human-Recognition. To stand in honor, one must honor one's Ancestors. One who does not honor one's ancestors dishonors self and one's people. However, one who holds Christianity as one's personal religion must specifically Renounce the Church instruction to kill all those who oppose The Church and Christianity, or one may not be accepted among Moors.

So I'm a Moor. How can I prove it?

See the next chapter, Chapter 4.

Chapter 4

How to Proclaim Nationality and Establish Non-US Citizenship

Nationality Proclamation For Everyone

Proclaiming one's nationality is a process, which everyone without an established nationality needs to do in order to be recognized in Law as Human and in order to freely navigate internationally. More than one method to establishing nationality exists. Some other's methods I share herein in parts. The Moorish American Institute's method I describe with blueprint accuracy.

The final goal to status correction and ability to navigate freely is to acquire an internationally-recognized document that recognizes nationality. First one needs to acquire a nationality document. This information is general for everyone born in America. Yet, I address the Moorish American status situation in particular as a matter of responsibility.

Nationality Document Part 2

A nationality document has criteria to meet in order to be considered lawful. For example, some government must approve it. Moorish Americans in a group have the ability to form Moorish American governments and to make such considerations. Those who desire to claim German, Anglo-Saxon, French, or Irish Nationalities, for examples, may not meet those nation's criteria. For example, Ireland requires proof of Irish citizenship of parent, grandparent, or great grand-parent. For those who do not have such proof, there is another proof to be had in the form of DNA test results. We have not yet heard of a nation that turns down DNA test results. For around $150, one may acquire a DNA test and results. Nevertheless, like other governments, Moorish American governments may make independent determinations as to who is Moorish American and who is not absent of DNA test results.

In addition and for the most part, anyone of any nationality, or citizenship may take on a new, or additional citizenship of a new nation, if such nation allows. For example, one friend has US, French, and British citizenship and all nations are fine with such. Whereas another friend renounced US Citizenship for Japanese citizenship. He is Moorish American by ancestry; however, his lawful nationality is now Japanese only, because in order to acquire Japanese citizenship, one must not simultaneously be a citizen of any other government. Never the less, the goals of this writing is to establish Nationality while remaining in America with full rights as either a National, or a Natural.

Nationality Proclamation for Naturals. We gather that some Moorish American organizations are still against granting citizenship to the Moorish American Nation to people of Non-Moorish American ancestries. However, most other nations do grant citizenships to others. Granting citizenship strengthens a nation. Granting a citizenship status through Naturalization grants an equal vote, voice, and ability to hold office, yet, cannot grant Blood-Rights to land. Such platform is pretty much the same across the board for all nations as all nations welcome and need others in order to strive to be the best that they can be. I ask those who disagree to give notable contrary examples.

WARNING: THIEVES IN THE TEMPLE

Several so called Moorish organizations offer fake nationality documents as authentic. One clue that gives them away is copy and paste. After collecting so much data from various Moorish American sources, one may easily determine that several are guilty of plagiarizing, trying to pass off copy-and-pasted material as authentic and unique documents. Another clue is redundancy. For example, the law only requires one federal legislative citation as proof. Citation is where one may find several instances of redundant copy-and-paste often surrounded by non-sense verbiage. If the material does not make sense, it is probably not the reader's fault.

WARNING: CHANGE OF FLAG

A claim to Moorish American Nationality without The Moorish American National Flag, which is the same as The Moor Empire Flag, is a claim different than The Moorish American Indigenous Claim, a massive strength already set in bedrock.

WARNING: LEARN OUTSIDE OF THE BOX

Do not settle for a nationality education from one Moorish source, or Moorish sources only. I encourage the reader to become familiar with other nation's nationality and naturalization laws and processes in order to see that nationality and naturalization processes are pretty much the same among most nations and so that one may become wise to other's tricks.

Acquiring a Moorish American Nationality Document

Preparation Steps. In preparation for Nationality Proclamation, a Moorish American must acquire an EL, or Bey title, and Non-Moor Bloods must acquire an Ibn EL, or Ibn Bey title. During the ceremony, one should wear a turban, or men may wear a red fes. The Moorish American Flag must be present and the ceremony may be conducted remotely, provided Moorish American Flags are visible through both connections.

The Nationality Ceremony must be conducted by a government official, or one officially appointed for the task. A Citizen-to-be must (a) **Renounce all other governments**, nations, and any other's claims, or restrictions over one. One must renounce oaths, vows, and allegiances that one made knowingly, or unknowingly. Renouncing cleans one's slate, so to speak, makes one able to lawfully, honorably, and freely give Allegiance. (b) **Give Word Of Allegiance**. As Moors, we give-our-word, which has to do with blood. Moors are not required to give oaths, vows, pledges, or swearings, which are religious rites. The Word Of Allegiance is short and to the point. (c) Witnessed. The ceremony must be witnessed by at least two humans. (d) The Document Certificate must be signed by the ceremony conductor. (e) The document must bare a government's seal.

The Word Of Allegiance should be given to The Moorish American Nation. Some may word such as; e.g., La Nación de Los Moros Americanos, or other international united construct. Moorish American is without specific need to also claim anything else; for examples, Tsalaki, Seminole, Ráramori, Mooron, Mooroon, or Blackfoot. However, one may include in one's nationality document such details.

The above information, a - e, is all that is needed for presentation, proof under most circumstances. Never the less, such presentations should contain at least an additional attachment page with cultural, historical, and lawful proof, describing Nation by Land, Flag, Symbols, and Ancestral Religion, for examples.

The Free National Appellation. The Free National Appellation, Moor Title, or Nomen, yet, not Name, which has to do with Christians, as taught by Prophet Noble Drew Ali, is composed of one's Personal identity, Family Surname, and Moor title, that is EL/El, or Bey. Personal identity, family surname, and Moor title are all recognized as The Appellation, one, unlike the Christian-name construct, which is first name, middle name, last name with suffixes such as Sr. and Jr, for examples. The Ali title is reserved for Royalty. Prophet Noble Drew Ali has instructed Moorish

Americans not to change their names, but merely to drop the middle name and suffixes, and replace one's El/EL, or Bey.

Hyphen -.   Some are unclear as to whether, or not to use a – hyphen; e.g., Smith-Bey, or Smith Bey, or Smith-El, or Smith El. Law dictates that a hyphen denotes that the word before the hyphen is more important than what follows. Noble Drew Ali did not use a hyphen. Therefore, The MAI recommends not using a hyphen. A surname without hyphen must be described as, for example, Smith Bey, or just Bey, or Smith may become a middle name for record's sake. For one's Title, use Titlecase, that is Lower and Uppercase Letters as Normal, as ALL CAPS removes one from human status.

Tribes.   The MAI's focus is on Nationality and Nationhood, yet, not on tribes, tribalism, or tribal matters.

Vestiges of Slavery.   Some feel that even though the middle name and Sr., Jr., are left off what remains is still a vestige, or mark of slavery, and argue that because of such, one should be free to rid one's self of any vestige of slavery and to choose a totally new identity. This is an argument that cannot be refuted and does not prevent one from Moorish American Nationality.

Proper Sources.   One's EL, or Bey title should come from a qualified and trusted Moor government and not be self-given. One may not want to find one's self dealing with courts of law and put on the spot with the question, "How'd you get that EL?" or "How did you get that Bey?"

Path to Human Status in Law

    Step 1: Constructing a Nationality Document. For all lawful and legal intents and purposes, the nationality document must announce that it is a nationality document, or it is not a nationality document. Wordings such as, *Proclamation, Affidavit*, and, *by Judicial Notice*, have power in certificate titles and should be included. The words, Affidavit and Judicial Notice, signify that the entire document serves as a proclamation of nationality. Judicial Notice is a rule that allows a fact to be introduced into evidence if the truth of that fact is so notorious, or well known, or so authoritatively attested that it cannot reasonably be doubted. Such is why The MAI recommends simple wording focused on only necessary claims.

    Once one possesses a Nationality Document, one's nationality has been recognized by one's own people, by one's own government, and filed with one's own government. No need to prepare and pay for so many CC mailings. However, we recommend zero to six external mailings.

    Step 2: To Notarize, or Not. One gets one's Nationality Document notarized, or not. Not having the nationality document notarized is perfectly fine for some purposes, such as the nationality process. However, for some office's requirements, a notarized document may be required, or at least make legal navigation smoother. If it matters, one may possess two documents, one un-notarized, the other notarized. A drawback may be a fee; however, banks notarize free for customers. As well, one may become a state notary. To find out how, check a state's website. The next steps in status correction are to get one's citizenship status recognized on all levels of external-to-Moors government, beginning with city, or county.

    Step 3: Registration with City, or County. At a city hall, or a county registrar, one needs to acquire a "Name Correction Form," or a "Name Change Form." The form will ask only three questions, simple questions that need only simple answers: (1) What is your current name/nomen? One should fill in one's name exactly as it reads on one's birth certificate, or certificate of live birth with periods, commas, suffixes and all. (2) What do you want your new name/nomen to be? This is where one drops middle name and adds EL, El, or Bey. And (3) Why do you want this change? One needs to answer to the effect of, "In order to proclaim nationality and to realign with my blood nation;" yet, not, "For religious reasons." ***Remember to remain focused on the process of nationality proclamation, not personal religion***.

    When one files a name change form, one should say to the man, or woman on the other side of the counter, "This is an attachment. I want you to attach this to the Name Change Form," and hand your <u>Nationality Proclamation Certificate</u>, or entire <u>Nationality Proclamation Document</u> to that man, or woman. This is one's chance to put on public record anything one wants. In a public publication, the provided information will run for 30-days, in which time, anyone has a lawful right to challenge. One who would challenge would need to provide proof against, not just disagree.

Once the 30-day wait is over, one visits a magistrate office and has a brief conversation with a magistrate, who cannot ask a question that an MAI graduate is unprepared for. The magistrate signs that paper filled out with the three questions and that paper receives an official office stamp. Next, one should tell the man, or woman who hands back that paper that one wants copies of that document including its attachments. Fees vary, yet, in Cuyahoga County, Ohio, for example, for $4 per page, one may receive copies of one's own nationality document with the county government seal stamped thereon. Such is proof on government record. Only one government proof is necessary.

Nationality documents enable one to present a lawful argument to change status; yet, do not change citizenship status. More steps are necessary.

1. Have regular and continuous interaction and learning with Moorish Americans for three years before applying for Citizenship.
2. Must be of age.
3. Demonstrate Moorish learning.
4. Be of good moral character.
5. Be mentally and physically fit.
6. Pay dues as taxes to a government of allegiance.
7. Not be convicted of a crime against The Moorish American Nation, or a Moorish American Citizen.
8. Give Word of Allegiance to The Moorish American Nation.

This Page is dedicated to Noble Drew Ali 1886-1929 Cc, an American Prophet

Fig 1   Symbol of Unity; A partnership among Moors and Europeans.

Must one claim Noble Drew Ali as a prophet in order to be recognized with Moorish American Nationality?

No. However, for those who may, what follows are some key reasons why one may claim Noble Drew Ali as an American Prophet.

Among American Moors, the Prophet and Master Moor educator, Noble Drew Ali, is the most prominent Ali. Ali was born on a Cherokee reservation in North Carolina and credited with (a) Establishing an education in nationality, (b) Constructing a Moorish American Land Trust, (c) In 1913 Cc reclaiming The Moor Empire Flag from US **President Woodrow Wilson 1856-1924 Cc**, (d) founding the civic organization, **The Moorish Holy Temple Of Science**, (e) founding the religious organization, **The Moorish Science Temple Of America** 1925 Cc, (f) founding **The Moorish Divine And National Movement**, November 29th, 1926 Cc, (g) authoring *The Holy Koran*, 1928 Cc with the *Circle 7* symbol on the cover, when there were no Qur'an translations in English. (h) founding the Religion, **Islamism**, and (i) Initiating the successful drive of 1928 Cc, which collected *144,000 Moorish American signatures* necessary to return The Moor Empire's Great Seal, The Pyramid Symbol, back onto the reverse side of the US Of A one-dollar note. For these reasons and more, Ali is regarded as an American prophet.

Each organization mentioned above is founded with the divine purpose, *To Help Uplift Fallen Humanity* through education primarily in Law, Civics, History, Culture, and Mathematics. [Civics: *relating to the duties or activities of people in relation to their town, city, or local area* (Oxford, 2004)]. The Prophet Noble Drew Ali set an eduction platform for Nationality Reclamation, High Culture Reintroduction, Social Improvement, Historical Restoration, and Spiritual Enlightenment, including the teachings of ISLAM, Zodiak Astrology, Yoga, BUDDHA, Kongfu Bey, JESUS, and All Prophets.

Step 4: Social Security Card. One goes to a Social Security Office and presents one's birth certificate, or certificate of live birth and name change form (name change form only, just the one page, no attachments) and requests a new social security card reflecting one's new and correct identity. A Social Security agent should inform that one may only be issued 10 Social Security Cards for life. (Such lets one know that one may change nationalities, or go back into subject status by choice, even after having gone through so much in order to proclaim Moorish American Nationality. Such should be encouragement to try something new).

Walking the Path of no Social Security Card.   For those seeking nationality-recognition and an international document without an already assigned social security number, some say that such is doable and may take years. If one has a path that takes less than five years, please share.

Step 5: Driver's License.   Even if one already has a driver's license, one is eligible for a new one that reflects the new identity. Wearing turban and/or fes, one goes to a Drivers Motor Vehicle with birth certificate, or certificate of live birth, name change form, and new social security card and acquires a driver's license. One has the freedom to on the driver's license, reserve one's Indigenous Rights by signing with one of the codes for *under duress*, which are, "u.d.," or, "..." at the end of the signature. Checking the box option, *Non-US Citizen National*, or some states have *Non-US Citizen Resident* for the same meaning, is a choice that simply with the stroke of a pen, opts one out of US Citizenship status.

A holder of a driver's license in the above-mentioned form, is officially no longer the US's citizen, one's nationality status is corrected to Human in National Law, and one possesses credentials that afford one travel ability, even internationally by land when combined with a birth certificate.

For international status correction, one needs an international document. The international document for most of us non-military people, is a passport. First we discuss the US Passport, because such is The MAI method, then we discuss other passports.

Step 6: Passport.   Once one has one's passport, one's nationality status is lawfully recognized as Human in International Law and all forms of government. To apply include: (a) an original copy of birth certificate, certificate of live birth, or other, (b) an Affidavit in support of the National Headdress for your turban, or fes (one needs to be part of a Moorish Government for this), (c) Name Change Form (without attachments), and (d) passport photos from a legitimate source. On the application, check all appropriate boxes to reflect Non-US Citizenship status for self and parents where appropriate. Non-US citizens have parents who are the same.

Return service can take up to 12 weeks, only up to six weeks with paying for express service (as of 2021 Cc).

Passport without a driver's license.   US Citizens and Non-US Citizens who can gain a passport, other than the World Passport, without a driver's license, or military ID, and birth records and social security number, or short of $50,000 USD, or five years minimum work should share such path. However, once a passport is acquired, the driver's license can be ended. See "Ending the Driver's License below."

States Are Countries

United States Of American States are actually single countries and territories with republik governments. MAI's Nationality and Citizenship Process establishes citizenship recognition with three governments, one with Moors, one with the US, and one with the country, or territory and republik, in which one was born. For example, a Moorish American, a True American, born in Texas becomes (a) a citizen of the Moorish American Nation, (b) a citizen of the Republik Of Texas, (not the State of Texas), and a Non-US citizen.

Reminder: Describing self as a Citizen of the US Of A is a worthy argument, because the US Of A is a Mooroccan government, as the reverse side of Moorish Science Temple Of America membership cards and the reverse side of the US dollar attest. Yet, the United States is not. Also, note that some argue that US Of A on temple membership cards means, United States Of Amexem, which can be an academic complication as well as a complication to the nationality proclamation process as an argument that need not be made for the goal at hand.

Other Passport Options

We discuss three of several options that can simply be purchased.

World Passport. A World Passport is a wonderful form of ID. A WP may be used as lawful ID within the US Of A, within other countries, and to cross international borders on land, even to return to the US \ Of A accompanied with a birth certificate, or certificate of life birth, and acceptable to fly within other countries; yet, not within the US Of A, or for international flights. The WP used in order to air-travel over multiple countries requires multiple in-country flights, then land-travel over international borders before boarding the next plane to the next border.
Driving, conducting a conveyance, is no problem with the World Passport. I have been pulled over by police in Canada and México, showed only my world passport (photo with fes), and nothing else was asked of me and nothing in addition is required. Paths off of the continent with the World Passport involves water.
One may acquire a world passport with, or without other identification.

The minimum proof of identity required in order to acquire a World Passport are two people with proper ID, who vouch for one's identity. The fee (as of now) for a 10-year World Passport is $125, $75 for a three-year World Passport. The World Passport affords one mobility, yet, does not correct citizenship status.

Other Nation's Passports.   Some Nation's sell their Passports.

Malta Passport.   The best passport to have is the Malta Passport, because the Malta Passport allows visa-free entry into more countries than the US Passport, including to all of the Americas. Acquiring a Malta Passport does not require one to hold a passport form anywhere else. The fee is $250,000 USD, the highest of all purchasable passports.

Peru Passport.   The Peru Passport allows visa-free entry to Austria, Belgium, Luxembourg, Netherlands, Germany, France, Spain, Portugal, Sweden, Finland, Denmark, Lithuania, Latvia, Estonia, Poland, Slovakia, Hungry, Italy, Greece, Czech Republic, Malta, Iceland, Liechtenstein, Norway, Switzerland, Monaco, San Marino, Vatican City, Ireland, Romania, Bulgaria, Croatia, Cyprus, and all South American nations except Venezuela. The fee is $50,000 USD, the lowest price for a nation's purchasable passport.

Ending the Driver's License

With the US Passport, Malta Passport, Peru Passport, or any nation's passport, one may allow one's driver's license to expire, if one desires, because such served its purpose and is no longer needed. Then if one is pulled over within the US Of A, US, or within any country, one need present nothing more than one's national passport.

What about Passports Created by Moorish Americans?

Moorish American Passports are good on any land controlled by Moorish Americans; however, in order to travel internationally, a Moorish American Passport carries no more weight than my East Cleveland, Shaw High School ID. If one wants to experiment with Moorish American Passports, fine, yet, I recommend having proper credentials just in case, because at international borders, one without proper, recognized, and verifiable credentials, will become stuck. I have been stuck in a foreign country before from trying some Moor's path that he probably never tried himself. I recommend asking for proof of path instead of becoming someone's lab rat, like me, whose proofs have come from walking rocky roads.

Totaling Fees Associated with MAI's method for establishing nationality and Correcting Status.

The First Cost: Time. The first cost to be considered in acquiring nationality-recognition is *Time spent on education*. MAI nationality education is three to nine weeks. With no more than a sixth-grade public school education, most adults are able to grasp MAI's nationality proclamation concepts. On the other hand, some people have spent and will spend years in order to sift through data and find the information needed in order to achieve the goal of nationality-recognition. Others will search their entire lives and fail to find this information. Without assistance, acquiring the proper education and required skills needed in order to form a new government and proclaim nationality through such government may take years more. Necessary skills are, but are not limited to, command knowledge of reading, writing, law, sciences, languages, history, culture, politics, art, art-design, advanced computer mastery, advanced software mastery, and social skills.

A Tip: Much Moorish learning comes only through social interaction. Therefore, befriending the right people, paying the right dues, making sure one is liked may be the only way to gain a Moorish American nationality education.

The Second Cost: Costs associated with Education. Costs associated with nationality education may be for class fees, transportation, books, and other learning materials, for examples. (Note: Learning courses should have a set number of classes, so that pupils may anticipate a graduation date and a time when they should be ready to exercise what has been learned).

Materials needed to run a Government Office.   Offices need seals, printers, paper, ink, computers, software, special paper, and more. Not everyone has to worry about these costs. For nationality proclamation documents and all certificates, paper should be 100% cotton and 20-pound weight, or heavier. Pen ink for signatures should be liquid gel. Liquid gel sinks into fibrous paper and prevents signatures from being smudged and altered.

Third Cost: Labor fee.   Paying for the construction of a nationality document. Some groups have people going $3,000-deep, or more in spending when all is said and done, with initial fees of hundreds of dollars, followed by monthly dues of $70, or more. On the other hand, for Nationality Document Construction and a nationality ceremony, The Sultanate Of Erie requires only a $30 donation, and $12 per year in dues. (***Note: Missing dues does not mean loss of nationality***).

Fourth Cost: Moorish American National ID.   All Moorish Americans need to be recognized and associated with a Moorish American government. Acquiring a Nationality ID from The Sultanate Of Erie requires a $25 donation.

Fifth Cost: Name Change.   Costs about $30. Getting a copy, about $12, is recommended, for a total of about $42.
Social Security.   No fee, yet, transportation and time are still costs.

Sixth Cost: Driver's License.   Driver's license fees vary nationwide, however, $30 seems average. Extra costs could be court costs, reinstatement fees, and taxes.

Seventh Cost: Passport.   A US Passport costs $150 for 12-week return service, $50 extra for express six-week service.

Associated cost with the US Passport.   (a) Certified Birth Certificate. One must provide a certified birth certificate. Costs vary nationwide and most states offer express service for an additional fee. The birth certificate fee is about $20 with express service around $10. (b) Photos, about $10.

What about those unable to attain Driver's License for Child Support, or other legal issues?

One may file for fee reductions, payment plans, temporary hold removals, negotiate for lower totals, especially if willing to pay about 30% all at once. Some local courts have an annual Amnesty Day, which provides a temporary window for people to fix such issues without fees. People who have good reasons for not wanting to pay court, traffic, and/or other legal fees and would rather write, call, show up, and in other ways fight, great, because as a Moorish American, such is one's right. I fought and it took years. A little money is not worth years of life being limited in mobility. In hindsight, I would have just paid. Such is my life-path and I would not walk any of it back, because now due to my suffering, I am able to help myself others. One must do what one thinks best for one's self.

TOTAL COST FOR STATUS CORRECTION (Normally)

One must decide for self. However, the MAI way is:	
Nationality Document Construction	$30
Moorish American National ID	$25
City/County Name Correction Filing Fee with one stamped copy (approximately)	$42
Driver's License	$30
Passport with express service	$200

GRAND TOTAL: $327

(All fees subject to change after April, 2023 Ce).

Who is eligible for Moorish American Nationality?

Any child born to a Moorish American father, mother, or grandparent is Moorish American by blood.

Who is eligible for Moorish American Citizenship

Any child born to a Moorish American father, mother, or grandparent is a Moorish American Citizen by blood. Aside from special circumstances, such as extreme *Worth to the Nation*, a foreigner applying for Moorish American Citizenship through The Sultanate Of Erie must fulfill the following requirements:

During the three-year naturalization process, one may obtain a Moorish American Institute Student ID Card, which is good for a legal and accepted second form of identification. One may also attain a Temporary Moorish American Nation Resident ID Card acknowledging one's own National Origins and one's commitment to The Moorish American Nation.

Do parents need to also pay for all of these services for each of their minor children?

No. Once a parent is registered as Moorish American, her/his children may be recognized as Moorish Americans via filling out and filing paperwork for correction and notification. Sultanate Of Erie fees for such are only for paper, printing, postage, and perhaps minimal processing, the total of which should not be more than about $20 per family provided one has learned through one's own process and can duplicate such for each child on one's own. If not, and one must rely on another, then fees could be costly. Simple Sultanate Of Erie registration for each child is $7, which goes to protection and insurance against fire, flooding, and theft. Moors unable to pay these Sultanate Of Erie Fees, will have all fees waved.

What happens with Citizens who do not pay dues for whatever reason?

The answer for National Citizens is different than the answer for others. Blood Nation Citizens cannot have their nationalities removed by anyone for non-payment of taxes. Anyone who says different is running a scam based on a mind-screw. However, one should pay dues/taxes, and/or make donations in order to build Moorish American National strength, which is the Moorish Americans. Moorish Americans should be able to barrow and to freely receive from their local governments. Never the less, a Blood National who does not pay dues/taxes, or make cash donations is still a part of and able to participate in government. The Sultanate Of Erie does not punish the poor. However, we need our government and our government needs us, so we encourage all to think needs.

Naturalized citizens should be happy to pay dues/taxes, make donations, pitch hands, put minds to work, and in all ways possible, help. Otherwise, why even try to join The Moorish American Nation? Naturalized Citizens may be deported, or left out.

Is there any other advise for helping one's self along this path?

Yes. Learn the value of respect, then cultivate relationships.

Why would a perfectly content European enjoying the privileges of White Status want to naturalize with Moorish Americans and become a Moorish American Citizen?

Individually, each would need to be asked. Yet, the main reason should be, In order to stand in honor in International Law. Some prefer being recognized as Human with an actual nationality among Noble Indigenous Humans, as opposed to being recognized as a subject of a foreign and occupying government corporation that is a company for profit, and has nothing to do with blood, or where one was born. Some have expressed concerns and fears of the US government failing. The rational is that cattle property would become the cattle property of the new government and the new government would require identification by nationality, not subject-class. The problem is that most, "Whites," do not have an actual nationality, so they would fall low in class-structure. Therefore, in order to fulfill the powerful idea and actual prophesy of Moors and Europeans rising together and never falling, several Europeans are pitching their hands, hearts, minds, and lots with Moorish Americans.

PSYCHOLOGICAL SUMMARY

There is a difference between, "I'm American," and, "I'm an American." The first is adjective and describes what one is like. The latter is a noun and says what one is.

I am Moor. I am a Moor. We say, "I am a Moor," and with that we are always saying, "I am Love," as well as identifying as a blood-member. On the other hand, notice the clumsiness of saying, "I'm a Moorish," versus the smooth, "I'm Moorish," or, "I'm Moorish American." The first sentence is without a noun, so the question remains, "A Moorish what?"

Remember that Moorish American is a national style that we, Moors of America, have adopted and under Prophet Noble Drew Ali's direction, adopted for all who join us whether as nationals by blood, or naturals by allegiance. Now those who say they are Moorish American comprise diverse groups with varying ideas on what Moorish American means, who Moorish Americans are, and where Moorish Americans come from with stories ranging from North America to Africa and all the way into outer space. Thus, a Moorish American follows a certain set of morals, some cultural and some religious, which anyone may follow, like a Kongfu move. Yet, one who claims to be a Moor takes a strong stance on blood as only a blood-member can. For example, Moors of America could decide next year to change national identification from Moorish American simply to Moors, Amooricans, Americans, Americanos, or Los Moros, for examples.

RECAP AND SUM FOR AMERICAN MOORS

If asked, "What are you?" You should say, "I am a Moor."

If asked, "What is your nationality?" you should say, "Moorish American."

If asked, "What is the land of the Moors?" you should say, "Amoorica, known as America."

If asked, "What is the Moor language?" you should say, "All of the Amoor languages," and that is enough to stand squarely.

WORKS CITED

Irving, Washington. (1894). *Chronicle of the Conquest of Granada. From the mass of Fray Antonio Agapida.*

Johnson, S. (1776). *A Dictionary of the English Language* in two volumes. London: Mifflin.

Oxford English Dictionary Volume IX. (2004). Simpson, J. A. & Weiner E.S.C. Oxford: Oxford UP.

Price, B. (2015). *The History of Chess in Fifty Moves.* Richmond Hill: Firefly Books.

Rogers, J. A. (1952, 1980). *Nature Knows No Color-Line, Research into the Negro Ancestry in the White Race Third Edition.* USA: Helga M. Rogers.

Webster's Comprehensive Dictionary Of The English Language, The New Interntional, Encyclopedic Edition (2006). Naples, USA: Trident International.

Webster, N. (1828). *American Dictionary of the English Language.* San Franscisco: Foundation for American Christian Education.

Whitehall, H. *Webster's New Twentieth Century Dictionary of English Language Unabridged.* (1956). Cleveland and New York: The World Publishing Company.

QUESTIONS, COMMENTS, PRODUCTS

For Questions and Comments to The Moorish American Institute, visit TheMoorishAmericanInstitute.org

For Questions and Comments concerning Moorish Psychology, address TheMoorishAmericanInstitue.org

For Products such as t-shirts with any of the following symbols (in color), see the PRODUCTS PAGE on TheMoorishAmericanInstitute.org

ABOUT THE AUTHOR

LONNIE BRAY EL, M. F. A., M.A. B.A., A.S., is a Master Teacher, Filmmaker, Writer, Communicator, Kongfu Master, Sword Master, and Intelligence Analyst, expert on Moorish and Anglo Histories, Court Records Procedures, Administrative Law - Indigenous Peoples, and Chess.

Bray EL authored, "The Book Of Moors," serves as headmaster of The Moorish American Institute, and hosts "Lonnie's Show." Bray EL's work is a catalyst for dialogue about Identity, Statelessness, and Culture, as well as Human-Trafficking, Bullying, and Integrity.

Bray EL's Honors include 22 National and International Film Awards, including for Best Director, Best Film, and Best Short Film; Poetry Awards, Schools And College Listings features "Lonnie's Blog" as a legitimate education source, and Bray EL is a Listee in "Marquis Who's Who in America."

Credentials
- Associate of Science Cum laude - Cuyahoga Community College.
- Bachelor of English | Creative Writing - Magna Cum laude - Cleveland State University.
- Master of Communications in Digital and Media Communications.
- Master of Fine Arts in Writing - Lindenwood University.
- Master of TESOL - Arizona State University.

Volunteer Work
- Writing, Filmmaking, and Martial Arts Instructor at City of Cleveland
- Director of the Moorish Psychology Association.
- Acting Sultan Of Erie.

www.ingramcontent.com/pod-product-compliance
Lightning Source LLC
Chambersburg PA
CBHW061837220326
41599CB00027B/5315

THE
ESOP
HANDBOOK
FOR BANKS

Exploring an Alternative for Liquidity and
Capital While Maintaining Independence

THE
ESOP
HANDBOOK
FOR BANKS

Exploring an Alternative for Liquidity and
Capital While Maintaining Independence

CORPORATE CAPITAL RESOURCES, LLC
www.ccrva.com

MERCER CAPITAL
www.mercercapital.com

THE ESOP HANDBOOK FOR BANKS

Exploring an Alternative for Liquidity and Capital
While Maintaining Independence

ISBN: 978-0-9825364-4-5

Peabody Publishing LP
5100 Poplar Avenue
Suite 2600
Memphis, Tennessee 38137
901.685.2120 (p)

Table of Contents

CHAPTER THREE: TAX CONSIDERATIONS

CHAPTER FOUR: VALUATION CONSIDERATIONS

CHAPTER FIVE: THE ESOP STOCK REPURCHASE OBLIGATION

CHAPTER SIX: LEGAL CONSIDERATIONS

CHAPTER SEVEN: ESOP INSTALLATION CONSIDERATIONS

APPENDIX A: Department of Labor ESOP Audit Checklist 71

About the Authors

About Corporate Capital Resources, LLC

About Mercer Captial

Introduction

The purpose of this handbook is to address an important omission in the current financial environment: the lack of a broader, strategic understanding of the possible roles of Employee Stock Ownership Plans, or ESOPs, as a tool for managing a variety of issues facing banks. Banks proportionately make more use of ESOPs than any other industrial classification in the U.S , often without understanding the extent of their potential applications. While an ESOP is not suitable in all circumstances, an ESOP may provide assistance in resolving the following issues, either by itself or in conjunction with other elements of a well-rounded strategic plan:

+ Augmenting capital, particularly for profitable institutions facing limited access to external capital. Though an ESOP strategy generally builds capital more slowly than a private placement alternative or a public offering, it provides certain tax advantages and may result in less dilution to existing shareholders;

+ Facilitating stock purchases by creating an "internal" stock market. The ESOP offers the further advantage of providing a vehicle to own shares that is "friendly" to the existing board of directors; and,

+ Providing employee benefits. ESOPs provide a beneficial tool in rewarding employees that add to the institution's long-term value.

ESOPs are subject to both tax and benefit (qualified plan) law provisions, which were first spelled out formally for ESOPs in the Employee Retirement Income Security Act of 1974 (ERISA).

The best decision tree will have a competent feasibility study performed to reduce the complexity to manageable proportions. ESOP implementation can be a complex process when viewed from a technical perspective. It need not be so complex when understood as part of a *coordinated* capitalization or market-making strategy. An ESOP alone is never *the* answer to a bank's strategy decisions, and ESOPs should not be installed without due appreciation of the need to coordinate the plan with key executive compensation, selling shareholders' desires, and a host of other concerns.

The need for strategic clarity may be illustrated by an anecdote based on our many years of working with ESOPs. In this example, an ESOP was rejected, though it could have been part of a good solution to the bank's needs.

An officer of the bank holding company (for a non-TARP bank) was interested in making a tax-efficient market for a class of preferred stock other than the existing common stock and was told by a tax attorney that the ESOP could only purchase the highest and best class of shares with respect to voting rights, dividend preferences, and other features.

While the "highest and best class" rule was correct and required, the counsel failed to suggest a broader strategy. The holding company could sell newly-issued common shares to the ESOP (which would be dilutive to per share value), gain a tax deduction for the purchase by the ESOP, and then use untaxed proceeds from the common stock sale to redeem some preferred shares (offsetting the dilution caused by the sale of stock to the ESOP). This process is at times referred to as "going public internally." In this case, the process could have been executed with minimal dilution.

This strategy for the closely held holding company would have required an independent valuation of the common stock and a coordinated plan, but would have provided the desired result: the redemption of preferred stock with pre-tax dollars using the ESOP as a single, tax-exempt shareholder.

This handbook describes the function of ESOPs in the real world of banks and bank holding companies. While it can correct misunderstandings and offer sound guidance, it cannot exhaustively detail the many interactions of Employee Stock Ownership Plans with current federal and state banking regulations and the extensive laws and regulations governing employee benefits and taxation. Bank directors and managers can use the information in this handbook to make solid, initial decisions regarding the potential merits of an ESOP.

Those directors and managers who make decisions affecting bank profitability, ownership, and capitalization should be aware of the potential advantages of an ESOP in offering a tax-advantaged vehicle that supports local control, while building shareholder value. This approach may prove beneficial compared with alternative structures that bring outside capital to the table for a price exacted in terms of greater dilution, dollars, and at times, control. Both approaches must be considered by any Board of Directors.

Before embarking on a particular strategy to deal with the various challenges facing small- to mid-size banks, the decision makers in profitable institutions may wish to consider how an ESOP can assist in addressing issues such as shareholder liquidity, employee ownership and compensation, and capital management.

CHAPTER 1

ESOPs AND THEIR BENEFITS FOR BANKS

An ESOP is a written, defined-contribution retirement plan—much like a more typical profit-sharing plan—designed to qualify for tax-favored treatment under IRC §401.[1] The assets in the plan (bank stock and other investments) are held in a tax-exempt trust. Participants ultimately pay ordinary income taxes on the value received when a vested account balance is paid to them.

A defined-contribution plan, such as an ESOP, does not guarantee what participants or beneficiaries will receive when a distribution is made to them. Further, the sponsor can define the amount of the contribution depending on its desire and ability to fund the plan each fiscal year in the context of the plan's liquidity needs.

The fundamental difference between an ESOP and a profit-sharing plan is that the ESOP must be "primarily invested in employer securities" as outlined in IRC §4975(e)(7); in short, it must own stock in the sponsoring company. How much stock an ESOP owns and when the stock is purchased are questions we will explore in subsequent sections of this handbook.

Why Do Banks Make More Use of ESOPs than Companies in Any Other Industrial Classification?

Closely held banks often need a mechanism to acquire shares efficiently. An ESOP permits containment of the number of stockholders through an untaxed mechanism ultimately under the governance of the board. Most bank ESOPs hold a minority interest in the employer's common stock. Banks which cannot buy back their shares directly can sponsor an ESOP to effect share purchases.

Who Can Sponsor an ESOP?

Since ESOPs must own shares in the sponsoring company, only C or S corporations (stock companies) can sponsor them. The laws permitting an ESOP to be an eligible shareholder in an S corporation have only come into being and been refined over the last decade. An S corporation ESOP behaves much differently than a C corporation plan.

How Does an ESOP Work?

The sponsoring bank or bank holding company makes contributions to an ESOP, either in stock or cash, subject to certain limits. These contributions are allocated among participants in proportion to compensation, or compensation plus length of service. The contributions to the plan and the assets in the plan must be allocated to the participants on a non-discriminatory basis. When an employee exits the plan, the ESOP may use its cash to purchase shares from the participant, often paid out over time, and those shares then are reallocated among the remaining participants. The ESOP is treated as a single, tax-exempt shareholder, which is beneficial for banks with shareholder counts approaching the number of shareholders that would trigger SEC registration.

How Does an ESOP Acquire Shares?

An ESOP may acquire shares using employer cash contributions, dividends or distributions on existing shares held in the plan, or by borrowing money to purchase stock of the sponsoring S or C corporation. The shares so acquired may be newly issued shares or purchased from existing shareholders or participants exiting the Plan. The employer may also issue shares to the plan in lieu of a cash contribution.

As an example, if a profitable bank contributes $100 to the ESOP, the ESOP can purchase $100 of newly issued shares at an after-tax cost to the bank of $60. Because contributions are tax-deductible, purchasing newly issued shares is accretive to total equity, although the transaction would dilute the ownership interest of non-ESOP shareholders. While an ESOP would be dilutive to non-ESOP shareholders in this example, it may be less dilutive than other alternatives (e.g., a private placement of common stock) that have less favorable tax or governance consequences for the bank.

When Does an ESOP Purchase the Sponsor's Stock?

The issue of when the sponsoring corporation's shares must be in the plan is not a bright line test. Many plans are operated as a "cash accumulator" for a year or two, using the tax-deductible contributions to build liquidity for a stock transaction. During this accumulation phase, there is no stock in the plan. In fact, since Limited Liability Corporations can sponsor qualified plans, it is possible for an LLC to sponsor a cash-only ESOP and become an S or C corporation in the following year or so to make stock available to the plan.

Any contributed accumulation of cash in an ESOP should be used within about three years to purchase shares of the sponsor (from whatever source) in order to meet the "primarily invested in employer securities" rule. A business plan for the ESOP should describe how the ESOP intends to acquire shares using the accumulated cash at no more than fair market value.

What Happens When an ESOP Borrows Funds to Purchase Stock?

Often, the transaction is structured with a "mirror" loan. In this case, the bank holding company would borrow funds from a third-party correspondent bank. The proceeds from this loan would be lent to the ESOP to purchase newly issued shares from the bank holding company or existing shares from outside shareholders. The ESOP then services its loan to the holding company using cash flow from contributions, dividends, or distributions, thereby providing funds to the holding company to service the correspondent loan. When an ESOP uses borrowed funds to acquire shares, the principal payments on the acquisition loan in essence are tax-deductible.

In a leveraged ESOP transaction, accounting rules generally require the bank holding company to record a "contra-equity" account in a like amount to the ESOP loan. This contra-equity account declines as the ESOP loan is amortized.

Thus, a leveraged ESOP transaction may be dilutive to the bank holding company's total equity.

How Does an S Corporation ESOP Differ from a C Corporation ESOP?

Among other distinctions, S corporation ESOPs do not face the tax liability that otherwise would "pass through" to taxable shareholders. For example, assume that an S corporation bank holding company reports taxable earnings of $100 and declares shareholder distributions of $40. In this scenario, a non-ESOP shareholder's tax liability is offset by his or her pro rata share of the holding company's distribution, leaving the shareholder with no "economic" dividend. However, the ESOP is tax-exempt. It would, therefore, retain its pro rata share of the company's distributions, which would be available to service debt, redeem shares from participants, or acquire additional shares.

What Is the Impact of TARP Executive Compensation Restrictions on ESOPs?

While Troubled Asset Relief Program ("TARP") requirements preclude key executives from non-qualified and discriminatory plans, these requirements do not apply to ESOPs.

What Benefits Do They Have for Participants?

Participants receive a retirement benefit as an equity interest in the sponsor at no cost to themselves. ESOPs typically reward loyal, long-term employees through vesting schedules, eligibility rules, and the like, which cause the bulk of the plan assets to accumulate in their accounts.

In What Instances Would an ESOP Not Be Appropriate?

ESOPs require a profitable sponsor possessing the ability to create value over time. Since they have an existing market for their shares, widely traded public corporations do not often use ESOPs. Highly leveraged ESOPs often are inadvisable. As a capital planning tool, ESOPs are less beneficial in situations where a bank or bank holding company faces the need to raise a significant amount of capital within a short time period. ESOPs provide significant benefits, but those benefits require patience to realize over time.

Who Controls the Stock?

For private corporations, the trustees are the legal owners who vote the stock, except in the case of major transactions, such as a sale of the bank or bank holding company. Participants in public company ESOPs vote all shares allocated to their accounts.

Who Should Be ESOP Trustees and What Are Some of Their Duties?

Anyone serving as a Trustee should have sufficient business experience and/or training in corporate finance and ESOP/ERISA requirements to make prudent decisions relative to the disposition of plan assets. The Trustees are the legal owners of the shares (not the employee participants) and vote the shares in closely held ESOPs in nearly all cases.

It is frequently the case in small ESOPs with a few hundred or less participants that a Trustee is also a Board member and/or a shareholder. This can create a conflict of interest if a shareholding Trustee wants to sell some stock to the ESOP. In such cases, the seller should abstain from all decisions related to the approval of a transaction at both the Board and Trustee levels, and the Board (which appoints Trustees) should also consider the appointment of a special independent Trustee to act as a consulting fiduciary relative to the stock purchase.

As a general rule, it is always wise for the board to consider bringing in an outside, independent Trustee for one-time transactions or longer roles when needed to provide independence and oversight, demonstrate regulatory compliance, and protect the existing fiduciaries. The latter can resume their roles following their abstention and the final decision. Such actions and the thorough documentation of them go a very long way towards protecting all parties in an ESOP transaction.

How Is Value Established?

The trustee establishes value. For privately held banks, the trustee engages an independent appraiser to value the stock, and the ESOP can pay no more than "fair market value" in transactions involving the plan. Valuing banks in the current regulatory and economic environment is challenging; banking industry and ESOP expertise should be key considerations for the trustee in appraiser selection. Appraisers consider numerous factors and apply specific valuation methods considered most appropriate. Draft regulations from the U.S. Department of Labor provide guidance specific to shares held by ESOPs.

What Are the Characteristics of a Successful Bank ESOP?

While every case is unique with respect to specific combinations of corporate objectives, employee benefit goals, tax concerns, and the like, the following considerations can help bank officers analyze the potential implementation of an ESOP:

+ A bank or a bank holding company that is a C or an S corporation can sponsor an ESOP, but it must be sufficiently profitable to take advantage of the tax benefits derived from contributions of stock or cash to the plan; corporations with less than $500,000 of pre-tax, pre-benefit plan earnings are questionable candidates.

+ The company must have sufficient employees to meet the various contribution limit and other tests required for compliance with IRS rules. ESOPs have been implemented in companies with fewer than 20 to 30 employees, but this is not recommended. An eligible payroll for qualified plan purposes of over $1 million is generally the threshold.

+ Both publicly traded and private corporations can sponsor ESOPs, but actively traded institutions typically do not need the market generated by an ESOP. Private and thinly traded companies often need the market for shares and make the greatest use of these plans. The suitable strategies and applicable rules governing ESOP operation differ considerably for private and public institutions.

+ Stock must be available within a few years of plan installation for either contribution to the ESOP or for purchase by the ESOP. The ESOP is indifferent to the source of the shares— newly issued shares or stock from outside shareholders—but it is an economic buyer and may purchase the shares at no more than fair market value. This stock value must be determined by an independent appraisal firm when closely held and thinly traded banks and bank holding companies are plan sponsors.

+ The financial strength of the bank should be sufficient over time to support shareholder value. Contra-indications of a strong ESOP candidate include: erratic or low earnings, inadequate capital ratios relative to regulatory expectations, poor CAMELS ratings,[2] and other negative factors known to management (e.g., pending detrimental litigation). It is important to remember that ESOPs are long-term retirement plans with an interest in the long-term economic viability of the sponsor.

+ A psychological factor is also important for management to consider. Bank management must be willing to engage in the process of managing not just cash flows, capital ratios, regulatory requirements, and the like, but also the interaction and effect of stock flows between the corporation, shareholders, and the ESOP. Such complexity can accomplish corporate objectives, but nonetheless requires effort and a clear understanding of the strategies involved.

+ A corollary of this ESOP "psychology" is the establishment of an ownership culture among the bank's employee base. Employees should be educated as to their influence on the value being created in the plan's stockholdings, and greater financial transparency may be necessary. It is important to note again that the ESOP participants have an economic interest in the value created but are not the legal owners or shareholders. The legal owners of the shares are the trustees of the plan, who are appointed by the Board of Directors.

ENDNOTES

1   Section 401(a) governs the qualification of all deferred compensation plans. The IRS has published a "A Guide to Common Qualified Plan Requirements at http://mer.cr/p1Q483.

2   Rating given by The Federal Deposit Insurance Corporation ("FDIC") and other bank supervisors to monitor the health of individual banks based on financials and on-site examinations. The acronym stands for: C - capital adequacy; A - asset quality; M - management quality; E - earnings; L - liquidity; S - sensitivity to market risk.

CHAPTER 2

USING AN ESOP TO ENHANCE CAPITAL

One of the benefits of an ESOP is the ability to raise additional capital by making tax-deductible contributions to the plan, which the ESOP can then use to purchase shares of stock from the sponsoring company. For example, a bank could contribute $100 to an ESOP, which because of the tax deductibility of the contribution, results in an after-tax expense of only $65 (assuming a 35% tax rate). Shortly thereafter, the ESOP can purchase $100 of newly issued common shares, thereby increasing the bank's common equity by $100 at an after-tax cost of $65.

Using this approach, over time the bank or bank holding company can enhance its capital. Taken a step further, the bank or bank holding company can use an ESOP as part of a strategy to redeem the TARP Capital Purchase Program ("CPP") preferred stock using pre-tax funds. This is not a direct purchase of the CPP preferred stock by the ESOP, but a redemption using holding company liquidity increased through the sale or contribution of common stock to the ESOP. We note, however, that an ESOP does not necessarily need to be used in isolation; instead, an ESOP can complement other strategies to enhance capital and redeem TARP or Small Business Lending Fund ("SBLF") preferred stock.

While an ESOP has benefits as part of a capital strategy, limitations exist on the strategy.

+ The benefits provided by the ESOP structure are realized gradually. If the bank or bank holding company requires an immediate capital infusion, the ESOP likely is not the best solution, although it can be used in conjunction with other capital raising strategies;

+ Quantitative limits exist on the amount the employer may contribute to the plan, thereby capping the capital enhancement and tax benefits derived from ESOP contributions;

+ The strategy requires the bank or bank holding company to be profitable (or at least to record a book tax benefit, if it reports a book loss) to realize the tax benefits; and,

+ The shares purchased by the ESOP must one day be repurchased from the plan's participants. As described in Chapter 5, these repurchase obligations can become significant issues in plans holding a more substantial share of the employer's outstanding common stock and should be managed carefully.

ESOPs and TARP/SBLF Obligations

The intersection of ESOPs, TARP, and SBLF provide an intriguing set of capitalization possibilities. Banks that accessed TARP, or that issued SBLF preferred stock to improve capital ratios or redeem the TARP preferred stock, may make use of an ESOP to assist in the retirement of these obligations. The key to using ESOPs as part of a capitalization strategy is to have a profitable banking institution with a CAMELS rating preferably of 1 or 2, but no worse than 3. Such banks can use tax-deductible ESOP contributions to build capital and do not have such significant capital limitations that an ESOP is inadvisable.

Since both the TARP and SBLF programs require after-tax dividends that eventually scale up to 9% annually, there is a significant need for after-tax dollars to service the required dividend payments, notwithstanding the need to redeem the securities. For example, a $10 million TARP preferred stock issuance currently requiring a 5% dividend means that the $500,000 after-tax annual distribution would require pre-tax income of $770,000 (assuming a 35% corporate tax rate) just to satisfy the current dividend obligation. The impending increase to a 9% dividend for our hypothetical bank with $10 million of TARP funds would then require $1.38 million of pre-tax earnings.

This rising dividend rate necessitates an ongoing assessment of alternatives to redeem the TARP preferred stock. Community banks with strong earnings should consider an ESOP within a capital planning framework and may find it advantageous relative to external capital markets that may provide capital on less-favorable terms.

SBLF Preferred Stock Redemption Using an ESOP

Assuming that a bank holding company converts its TARP preferred stock into SBLF preferred stock, the dividend "step-up" date would be extended by four and one-half years and, depending on the bank's loan growth, the dividend rate may be reduced below TARP's 5% dividend rate. The bank holding company can use the period prior to the SBLF's dividend rate increase to accumulate cash inside the ESOP. This requires tax-deductible contributions to the ESOP, building an off-balance sheet pool of liquid assets that we refer to as a "cash warehouse."

For example, if the bank has the capacity to make pre-tax contributions of $1 million annually for three years (while the SBLF is in place) without impairing capital ratios, at the end of the three years the bank holding company could sell newly issued shares to the ESOP and recover the $3 million. The $3 million of capital obtained through the ESOP transaction could then be used to reduce the SBLF preferred stock.

After purchasing stock from the bank holding company, the ESOP's liquidity could be replenished with both dividend income and future contributions from the sponsoring bank to repeat the process. The elimination of the dividends on the repurchased SBLF preferred stock will also improve the bank holding company's cash flow. The process would take some time, but the ESOP would benefit employees and would comprise a single, locally controlled shareholder, instead of the multitude of dispersed shareholders that may result from a private placement.

To achieve the same result with after-tax earnings, assuming a 35% state and federal tax rate, the holding company would need to allocate $4.6 million of pre-tax earnings. The tax arbitrage resulting from using an ESOP yields a $1.6 million improvement relative to a strategy using after-tax earnings to redeem the preferred stock. Stated somewhat differently, the holding company would have an additional $1.1 million of capital at the end of the three-year ESOP implementation period than if it simply redeemed the SBLF preferred stock using after-tax earnings ($3,000,000 contribution multiplied by the 35% tax rate).

Is this financial benefit sufficient to warrant the costs of plan implementation and dilution to existing shareholders? If the bank desires to keep governance a local matter and use the ESOP to augment, not entirely replace, other strategies the answer is often "yes." In some cases, the issue of whether to implement an ESOP requires an analysis of the relative valuations of stock issued to an ESOP or through a private placement and the dilution expected under both scenarios.

Example of an ESOP Transaction

To illustrate the benefits of using an ESOP as a capital-raising tool, we present a simple example of a bank that installs an ESOP with the goal of using tax-deductible contributions to the plan eventually to redeem its TARP CPP preferred stock. While we present specific numbers below, we emphasize the general impact on bank and company capital ratios, cash flows, stock value, and ownership transition.

XYZ Bancorp

For this example, we consider a healthy financial institution, XYZ Bancorp, with TARP preferred stock totaling approximately 1% of its assets, or $5 million. The holding company's primary asset is its investment in XYZ Bank, and it incurs minimal operating expenses. At December 31, 2011, both the bank and the holding company are well-capitalized, but management of XYZ Bancorp has set a goal to redeem the TARP preferred stock by December 31, 2014, before the dividend rate increases from 5% to 9%.

Additionally, XYZ Bank has a management team that is nearing retirement age and that owns a meaningful percentage of the company's closely held shares. After evaluating a number of options, the management team determines that installing an ESOP is the most effective way to accumulate cash with which to redeem the TARP preferred stock and also to transition ownership to the next generation of management while facilitating the repurchase of shares held by the existing management team.

ESOP Transaction

The ESOP is installed effective January 1, 2012, and the bank makes tax-deductible ESOP contributions of $1,666,000 in 2012, 2013, and 2014. The ESOP, in turn, accumulates these cash contributions until 2014, when it purchases $5 million of newly issued common shares in XYZ Bancorp. As the last step in this transaction, XYZ Bancorp redeems the TARP CPP preferred stock investment with the funds provided by the ESOP's purchase of newly issued common shares.

The contribution, which is significant at approximately 25% of covered compensation, causes XYZ Bank's return on assets to decline by about 20% during the 2012 to 2014 period, versus a scenario where no ESOP is implemented assuming the bank makes no offsetting adjustments to any existing benefit plans. From a capital standpoint, we compared XYZ Bank's equity/asset ratio in 2014, assuming ESOP implementation occurs, to an alternative scenario that does not establish an ESOP but assumes a $5 million dividend from the bank to the holding company. In this comparison, XYZ Bank's 2014 equity/asset ratio is about 3% higher if the Bank uses an ESOP.

In 2014, the ESOP purchases shares of the company's common stock at the fair market value of the stock as determined by an independent appraiser. The shares purchased by the ESOP in 2014 are newly issued by the company, raising the additional capital necessary for management in turn to redeem the TARP preferred stock. An important issue for the ESOP's independent appraiser to consider is the extent to which XYZ Bank's contributions leading up to the ESOP's share purchase are indicative of its ongoing contribution levels. The example assumes that, following the ESOP transaction, ESOP contributions normalize from 25% to 10% of compensation. Based on this assumption, the total number of shares outstanding increases by approximately 9% in our example, and the ESOP now holds around an 8% stake in the company, but the TARP Capital Purchase Program preferred stock has been redeemed and the dividend payment obligation extinguished without raising external capital.

Why would management and the Board of Directors determine that such dilution to earnings, capital ratios, and ownership is an acceptable result? In short, it would reach this conclusion if these outcomes compare favorably relative to the alternatives available:

+   Relative to a scenario where no ESOP is installed, but XYZ Bank provides a dividend of $5 million to enable XYZ Bancorp to redeem the TARP CPP preferred stock, the ESOP scenario results in greater capital at the bank and holding company. This additional capital approximates the tax benefit of the ESOP contributions.

+   Investor groups unaffiliated with the holding company may require substantial concessions to encourage their investment, which may be dilutive to remaining shareholders (e.g., warrants in addition to the shares purchased). While an ESOP can pay no more than fair market value for the shares, it may be viewed as a more friendly vehicle to acquire shares than a private investor group.

Alternative to an ESOP

As an alternative to installing an ESOP, XYZ Bancorp management may raise additional capital in a 2014 private placement transaction. Assuming no other changes to financial performance, management may expect the private placement to result in greater dilution of the common stock. For example, existing shareholders and directors may not have the financial means or desire to make substantial additional capital injections. In this case, the bank holding company may turn to an investor group to raise the necessary capital; however, smaller banks often attract less interest from these groups, who often look for attractive public offering or acquisition candidates. With a less persuasive exit strategy, the investor group may demand greater concessions on price, transaction enhancements such as warrants, and other non-financial perquisites such as board of directors' seats. Based on these requirements from investor groups, management may reasonably expect that the number of shares the ESOP would need to purchase in order to raise enough capital to redeem the TARP would be smaller than the number of shares that would need to be sold in a private placement.

In the example, we assumed that XYZ Bancorp issues stock in a private placement at an approximate 15% discount to the shares' fair market value, as would be used in an ESOP transaction. If this occurs, then the bank holding company would issue more shares to the investors in the private placement than it would have issued to an ESOP, creating greater dilution for all the shareholders. Depending on the ongoing ESOP contribution, by implementing an ESOP, the bank holding company could have a higher earnings per share than if it undertook a private placement and provide its employees with an additional retirement benefit.

Scenario Comparison

The following tables summarize certain key metrics for XYZ Bank under the four scenarios described above. All scenarios assume the same growth and profitability expectations.

Do Nothing	2011	2012	2013	2014
Earnings				
ROAA - Company	0.97%	1.00%	1.00%	1.00%
ROAE - Company	9.92%	9.91%	9.45%	9.08%
Net Income - Consolidated	$5,525	$5,801	$6,091	$6,396
Performance Metrics				
Earnings per Share	$100	$105	$110	$116
Book Value per Share	$931	$1,026	$1,125	$1,229
Shares Outstanding	55,250	55,250	55,250	55,250

Bank Dividend	2011	2012	2013	2014
Earnings				
ROAA - Company	0.97%	1.00%	1.00%	1.00%
ROAE - Company	9.92%	9.91%	9.46%	9.44%
Net Income - Consolidated	$5,525	$5,801	$6,091	$6,396
Performance Metrics				
Earnings per Share	$100	$105	$110	$116
Book Value per Share	$931	$1,026	$1,125	$1,139
Shares Outstanding	55,250	55,250	55,250	55,250

ESOP	2011	2012	2013	2014
Earnings				
ROAA - Company	0.97%	0.79%	0.80%	0.81%
ROAE - Company	9.92%	7.98%	7.86%	7.74%
Net Income - Consolidated	$5,525	$4,718	$5,008	$5,313
Performance Metrics				
Earnings per Share	$100	$85	$91	$92
Book Value per Share	$931	$1,007	$1,086	$1,072
Shares Outstanding	55,250	55,250	55,250	60,342

Private Placement	2011	2012	2013	2014
Earnings				
ROAA - Company	0.97%	1.00%	1.00%	0.94%
ROAE - Company	9.92%	9.91%	9.46%	8.60%
Net Income - Consolidated	$5,525	$5,801	$6,091	$6,396
Performance Metrics				
Earnings per Share	$100	$105	$110	$110
Book Value per Share	$931	$1,026	$1,125	$1,108
Shares Outstanding	55,250	55,250	55,250	61,017

The tables indicate the following:

+ The "do nothing" strategy generates the most favorable financial metrics, but it also does nothing to eliminate the TARP or SBLF preferred stock and the dividend step-up that would occur and absorb a greater proportion of the bank holding company's earning power;

+ The private placement strategy generates the highest pro forma capital ratios, but at a cost of greater dilution to existing shareholders and, potentially, a loss of control; and,

+ The ESOP strategy generates better capital ratios relative to a strategy whereby the bank holding company uses the bank's existing equity to redeem the TARP or SBLF preferred stock. Further, when ESOP contributions normalize from their initial rate of 25% of compensation, the ESOP transaction generates better or comparable EPS to a private placement, but has the salutary benefit of providing additional compensation to the employees.

The ESOP Going Forward

Once the bank has used the cash held by the ESOP to raise capital with which to redeem the TARP CPP preferred stock, the ESOP can be used to buy out existing shareholders desiring liquidity. XYZ Bancorp pays annual dividends on its common stock, which results in dividends paid to the ESOP. Additionally, management can continue to make contributions to the ESOP. The dividends and the ongoing contributions result in cash inflows for the ESOP, which coupled with any cash remaining after the TARP redemption, leaves the ESOP with cash available to purchase additional shares in later years, increasing the ownership percentage. Keep in mind that the shares purchased after 2014 are obtained from existing shareholders, and the only dilution occurs in 2014 with the issuance of new stock to redeem TARP.

This can continue indefinitely (or at least until the ESOP owns 100% of the company), with the company varying the amount of contributions and dividends depending upon the amount of shares the ESOP wishes to purchase, the financial performance of the bank, and the liquidity needs of other shareholders. The contributions are deductible for tax purposes, while the dividends are not. Shareholders who are not participants in the ESOP are not able to participate in the contributions, only the dividends, and management must take into consideration the need to balance the return to all ownership classes of the company. Additionally, all else equal, the contributions do result in a decline in earnings in the years in which they are made, and the reduced earnings must be balanced with the benefits of creating liquidity for shareholders and increasing the ESOP's ownership interest.

Additional Considerations

The example above involving XYZ Bancorp made a number of simplifying assumptions for illustrative purposes. In reality, additional complexities enter into any analysis as to whether an ESOP satisfies a company's objectives. Some of these additional considerations include:

+   If net income is depressed leading up to the ESOP transaction as the company builds a "cash warehouse" by making periodic ESOP contributions, the stock value at the time of the transaction may be reduced, reflecting the depressed earnings. However, depending on the specific facts and circumstances, an appraiser may not consider the amount of such contributions to be reflective of the company's actual expense structure and may factor this consideration into the determination of the company's stock value at the time of the transaction. Some add-back of plan contributions in excess of peer-group retirement plan contributions is common when arriving at a representative earnings base for a valuation.

+   The example shown here pertaining to XYZ Bancorp shows a decline in earnings in the years in which the ESOP contributions occur, reflecting an increase in personnel expenses in the amount of the contributions. In some situations, the increase in expenses may not be as significant. Because ESOP contributions represent an employee benefit, banks with ESOPs may consider reducing contributions to other retirement plans or may otherwise reduce certain personnel expenses as an offset to the ESOP contribution. The extent to which ESOP contributions increase total expenses depends on the sponsoring bank's overall strategy for balancing the various needs and objectives of the bank.

+ In the preceding example, we assumed that balance sheet growth would be identical under all scenarios. However, because the ESOP may provide a greater amount of capital over time, the sponsoring bank may be able to realize greater balance sheet growth in the long term, thus enhancing shareholder value. For example, by using the ESOP to provide shareholder liquidity, more shares remain outstanding, relative to an alternative of repurchasing shares into treasury and thereby reducing common equity.

CHAPTER 3

TAX CONSIDERATIONS

Tax-qualification is an attribute bestowed on an employee benefit plan by the IRS. This status allows the plan sponsor to make contributions to the plan using pre-tax dollars, within certain limits, and also allows the income tax on the participants' benefits to be deferred until the benefits are actually received by the participant or the beneficiary.

For an ESOP to retain its tax-qualification, the plan must be designed and operated in compliance with IRS and ERISA (Department of Labor) regulations.[1] These rules were written, for the most part, to ensure that plans do not discriminate in favor of highly compensated employees, and that plans are administered to protect the rights and benefits of plan participants. Employers must utilize experienced professionals to assist with plan operations and compliance in light of the complex body of interrelated IRS and DOL regulations.

C Corporation ESOPs

The following schematic shows the relationship between a C corporation bank holding company, the ESOP trust, the employees, and other shareholders. This example depicts the ESOP's purchase of stock from existing shareholders.

THE C CORPORATION ESOP

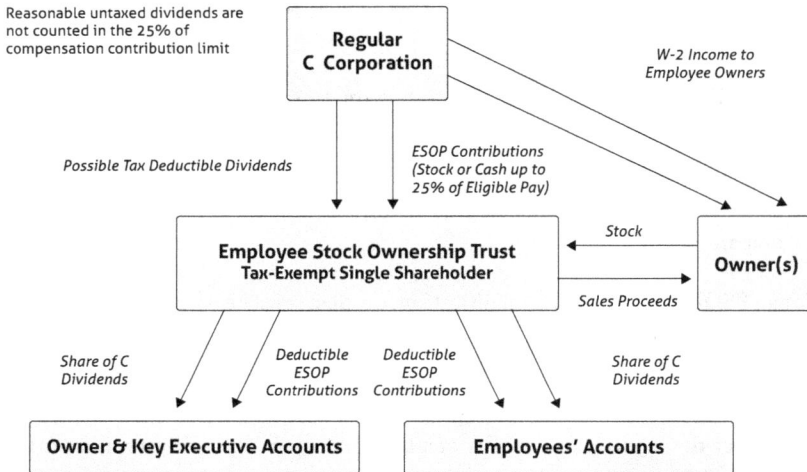

Reasonable untaxed dividends are not counted in the 25% of compensation contribution limit

Regular C Corporation

W-2 Income to Employee Owners

Possible Tax Deductible Dividends

ESOP Contributions (Stock or Cash up to 25% of Eligible Pay)

Stock

Employee Stock Ownership Trust
Tax-Exempt Single Shareholder

Owner(s)

Sales Proceeds

Share of C Dividends

Deductible ESOP Contributions

Deductible ESOP Contributions

Share of C Dividends

Owner & Key Executive Accounts

Employees' Accounts

This simple arrangement depicted above of a direct sale of stock from an existing shareholder to the ESOP is common for small blocks of stock for which the purchase can be funded by cash accumulated in the plan.

ESOP transactions can become more complicated, however. For instance, to purchase shares beyond its existing liquidity resources, the ESOP may use debt in a so-called leveraged ESOP transaction. In one variation of this transaction, the bank holding company would borrow funds from another bank, and the bank holding company would then loan the funds to the ESOP via a mirror loan. The bank holding company and potentially the seller of the shares acquired by the ESOP would guarantee the third-party bank loan. The ESOP would then make debt service payments on the "mirror" loan to the bank holding company, which would then service the third-party bank debt.

C corporation banks and bank holding companies with a large number of shareholders will often have different strategies for stock purchases than S corporations, since more than one class of stock may exist.

A major advantage of private C corporation ESOPs that is not available for S corporation ESOPs is the ability of a shareholder who has held his or her shares for three years or more to take advantage of a tax-free sale of stock to the ESOP in an IRC §1042 tax-free (tax-deferred) rollover.

An owner of a closely held C corporation can defer capital gains taxation on stock he or she sells to an ESOP if:

+ The ESOP owns 30% or more of each class of outstanding stock or of the total value of all outstanding stock, excluding nonconvertible, nonvoting preferred stock; and,

+ The seller reinvests ("rolls over") the sale proceeds into qualified replacement property (stocks or bonds of domestic operating companies) during the period from three months before to 12 months after the sale.

Currently, the definition of qualified replacement property ("QRP") includes U.S. stocks, bonds, debentures, other certificates of indebtedness and convertible securities, if they are securities of companies incorporated in the U.S. Investments that are not qualified include U.S. government and municipal bonds, mutual funds, and real estate investment trusts ("REITs").

The money rolled over into replacement property need not be the actual proceeds from the sale, but can be an equivalent amount of money from another source. Any or all of the proceeds can be rolled over, and the seller(s) will pay taxes only on the portion that is not rolled over. Two or more owners may combine their sales to meet the 30% requirement if the sales are part of a single, integrated transaction. It has become increasingly common in section 1042 transactions for sellers to facilitate the sale of stock to an ESOP by pledging part or all of their replacement property as collateral for a loan to fund the transaction, especially in companies with limited assets or with substantial debt.

None of the shares sold to the ESOP in a transaction to which section 1042 applies may be allocated to ESOP accounts of the seller, certain relatives of the seller (ancestors, siblings, spouse, or lineal descendants), non-selling shareholders holding more than 25% of company stock, or family members of the more-than-25% shareholders if they own stock by attribution (e.g., spouses). This restriction does not apply to ESOP stock not purchased in the rollover transaction. There is one exception to these restrictions: lineal descendants of the selling shareholder(s) may be allocated a total of 5% of the stock, provided that the lineal descendants are not treated as more-than-25% shareholders by attribution.

The section 1042 rollover also requires that the selling shareholder(s) must otherwise be eligible for capital gains treatment on the sale and cannot have received the stock through exercising stock options or certain employee stock award programs. The stock should be held by the ESOP for at least three years from the date of sale; if the ESOP disposes of the shares within three years after the sale, the employer generally must pay a 10% excise tax on the proceeds from the disposition. This can be a negative factor when considering a later sale to an outside buyer, an IPO, or a "roll-up" transaction.

Some larger transaction amounts (typically greater than $5 million) are rolled over into floating rate notes with long-term (50 years or more) corporate bonds as the QRP. Up to 90% of the bond value can be borrowed and reinvested without constraint. Although investors considering this approach should proceed with caution in light of their real needs, this strategy may work for a younger investor with good money management and time available to grow the 90% more than the original 100% of the proceeds could grow in a buy-and-hold portfolio.

Sellers using the section 1042 rollover often avoid taxation completely by retaining the replacement property until death, at which time the property transfers to their heirs with a stepped-up basis. With capital gains taxes currently at historic lows and significant uncertainty regarding future capital gains tax rates, the taxable options to the tax-free rollover should be well understood before committing to a 1042 deal. A good ESOP feasibility study will exhaustively treat both taxable and untaxed transactions.

S Corporation ESOPs

An S corporation is a "pass-through" entity, in which the individual shareholders are responsible for the income taxation attributable to their pro rata portion of the bank or bank holding company's earnings. The ESOP, like any other S corporation shareholder, participates in the profits and losses of the sponsoring corporation. The ESOP receives its proportionate share of any earnings that are distributed at the direction of the Board, computed on a per-share, per-day rule in the tax year under consideration. Since an S corporation ESOP is treated as a single shareholder and pays no taxes, the earnings on S corporation shares are not taxable. They flow untaxed into the plan and can be used to purchase additional shares or pay down a stock acquisition loan.

This effectively means that the S corporation ESOP can be more tax-efficient than its C corporation counterpart. At the extreme end of the ownership spectrum, i.e., an ESOP owning 100% of the employer's common stock, the only shareholder is the ESOP Trust, which pays no taxes. There is no need to distribute earnings on shares to taxable shareholders to cover their tax obligations, and the sponsoring S corporation is effectively tax-exempt. The number of such companies is increasing, although outside of the banking industry.

In the following diagram, we have shown a simple example in which the ESOP purchases stock directly from an existing shareholder using funds from the plan (either from cash accumulated in the plan or via a seller note making periodic principal and interest payments to the seller).

THE SUBCHAPTER S ESOP

The ability to use untaxed dividends means that the limiting factors in most stock purchases are the earnings capacity of the corporation and the ESOP ownership percentage.

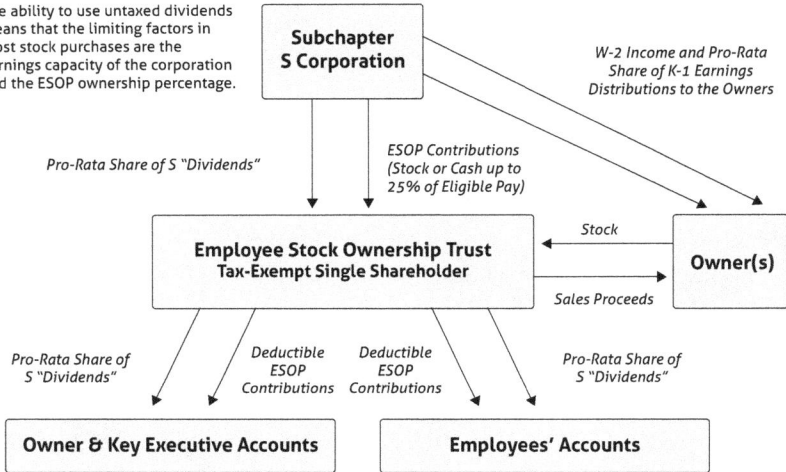

Subchapter S Corporation

W-2 Income and Pro-Rata Share of K-1 Earnings Distributions to the Owners

Pro-Rata Share of S "Dividends"

ESOP Contributions (Stock or Cash up to 25% of Eligible Pay)

Employee Stock Ownership Trust
Tax-Exempt Single Shareholder

Stock

Owner(s)

Sales Proceeds

Pro-Rata Share of S "Dividends"

Deductible ESOP Contributions

Deductible ESOP Contributions

Pro-Rata Share of S "Dividends"

Owner & Key Executive Accounts

Employees' Accounts

If the company reports earnings of $1 million and the ESOP owns 50% of the shares, the non-ESOP shareholders, who own the remaining 50% of the stock, would be responsible for the taxes on $500,000 of the company's earnings. The ESOP would not be responsible for any taxes on earnings. A distribution of 35% of earnings to the taxable shareholders to satisfy their income tax obligations would require the same distribution to the ESOP of $175,000. This is a much more efficient method of recovering tax dollars than a simple deductible contribution to an ESOP.

To achieve a recovery of tax dollars equal to $175,000 with a pre-tax contribution of either stock or cash to an ESOP, the required contribution at an assumed 35% state and federal tax rate would be about $270,000. In the case of our 50/50 ownership split between the ESOP and non-ESOP shareholders, the company still distributes cash in the amount of 35% of $1 million, but in this case the ESOP share represents a complete recovery of dollars otherwise lost to taxation.

Despite the substantial benefits of using an ESOP with a large ownership interest to improve cash flow in S corporations, this strategy may be difficult to implement for several reasons. First, the other shareholders want to partake in the earnings. But, more importantly, it takes significant time (typically more than 10 years) for a company to buy in a significant proportion of its shares – even with a full tax shield for the ESOP purchase. Additionally, when an ESOP uses a loan to purchase shares, the debt may be treated as a reduction of shareholders' equity. In accounting terms, this contra-equity account arises because the accounting rules treat the leveraged transaction as if it were a repurchase of stock. While the contra-equity account declines over time as the debt is repaid, the transaction would dilute the holding company's capital ratios at the outset. Lastly, ESOPs owning large proportions of the employer's outstanding securities may generate another set of problematic issues, because of the materiality of the obligation to repurchase shares from participants exiting the plan.

There also are some concerns with partial S corporation ESOP ownership and high levels of corporate earnings. For example, if our example ESOP above only had 40% of the stock and the outside 60% owners wanted 70% of earnings distributed, the ESOP's share of the $1 million of earnings would be 40% of $700,000, or $280,000. That could represent more cash than the ESOP needs for share purchases, loan payments, or repurchases of shares from departing, vested account balances.

Some S corporation banks with partial ESOPs have inadvertently "overfunded" their plans, making for some large participant accounts, when the distributions paid to outside shareholders have been quite high. This is not common, but represents one of many design considerations when implementing an ESOP.

Additionally, terminated participants may have vested account balances in the ESOP still held in the form of bank shares; the presence of stock in terminee accounts could benefit both from distributed earnings on their S corporation shares as well as price appreciation in the underlying shares The effect of growing account balances for terminated participants is not difficult to deal with but needs to be understood both in the design and ongoing operation of an ESOP.

Very small S corporation ESOPs face an additional concern that C corporation ESOPs do not: the IRC §409(p) "anti-abuse" rules. After the passage of legislation in 1998 permitting ESOPs to be eligible shareholders in S corporations, the IRS belatedly recognized that there was a potential for abuse. The concern was that, the ESOP would not share ownership broadly on a non-discriminatory basis, yet would provide a full tax exemption to the shareholders/participants who may be the same individual(s).

Since any S corporation with all of its shares held in the tax-exempt trust is effectively an untaxed operation, a small company with few employees could hold its earnings on the untaxed balance sheet of the company with that wealth concentrated in a few hands. The IRS, concerned with such a massive tax shelter, wrote the anti-abuse rules to prevent such a concentration of ownership. Without adducing the technicalities of this law, a failure to meet this requirement effectively destroys the ESOP, through a 50% excise tax on the amounts held by "disqualified persons," possible disqualification of the plan, or other negative effects.

Although there are ways of addressing the ownership concentration issue, S corporation companies with fewer than about 15 participants in an ESOP, or with a potential of declining to that level, should either be a C corporation or consider an alternative to the ESOP.

Limits on ESOP Contributions

For an ESOP, as for any other tax-qualified plan, the IRS imposes limits on the amount of tax-deductible contributions. For eligible participants, typically those working at least 1,000 hours per year and age 21 or older (though sponsors can be more generous), the contribution by the sponsor to all of the qualified plans cannot exceed 25% of "covered" compensation. For example, a bank with an eligible payroll of $2 million, making employer 401(k) contributions of $100,000, could contribute a maximum of $400,000 to an ESOP on a tax-deductible basis. (Total allowable contribution of 25% of $2 million = $500,000. Netting out the 401(k) contribution of $100,000 leaves $400,000 for the ESOP.)

While historically other contribution limits have been subject to a cost of living adjustment, there have been no increases for the past two years.

The following caps apply for the 2011 and 2012 plan years:

	2011	2012
Compensation limit for computing all plan contributions *Source: Annual Compensation - IRC 401(a)(17)/404(l)*	$245,000	$250,000
Maximum 401(k) elective deferral *Source: Elective Deferrals - IRC 402(g)(1)*	$16,500	$17,000
Age 50 401(k) catch up contribution maximum *Source: Catch-up Contributions - IRC 414(v)(2)(B)(i)*	$5,500	$5,500
Annual addition limit without 401(k) catch up amount *Source: Defined Contribution Limits - IRC 415(c)(1)(A)*	$49,000	$50,000
Annual addition limit with 401(k) catch up above age 50	$54,500	$55,500

COLA increases for dollar limitations on benefits and contributions are updated annually and reported on the www.IRS.gov website each fall.

It must be noted that ESOPs have some exceptions to the above constraints. For example, the following additional monies flowing untaxed into an ESOP do not count in any of the above limits:

+ S corporation earnings on shares held by an ESOP (which can be used to purchase and repurchase shares or pay down an ESOP loan), and,

+ C corporation dividends that are characterized as reasonable by the IRS.[2]

The effect of these exceptions for ESOPs is that the contributions to ESOPs generally run well ahead of other profit-sharing plans. For example, the average employer contribution to a 401(k) is about 4% of compensation. We have seen ESOPs in some cases with total funds flowing into participant accounts averaging 35% or more of eligible pay in some years, though the national average is closer to 8%. The typically high level of plan contributions eventually results in substantial stock values accumulating in participant accounts, making the ESOP a great tool to build retirement savings.

ENDNOTES

1   The Employment Retirement Income Security Act of 1974.

2   IRC Section 404(k)(5)(A).

Summary of Similarities and Differences Between S and C Corporation ESOPs

Feature	Private C Corporation ESOP	Subchapter S ESOP
ESOP 1042 Tax-Free Rollover	Yes, if ESOP = 30%	No
Tax-Deduction Limit for ESOP Loans	Includes only Principal in Most Cases. Must Pass "One-Third" Test for This. Otherwise, the Limit Includes Principal and Interest	Counts both Principal and Interest
Tax-Deductible Dividends	Yes, if "Reasonable" and Used to Retire ESOP Debt, Passed Through to Participants or Reinvested in Shares	No
Untaxed Earnings on ESOP Shares	No	Yes
Dividends Can Be Distributed to Participants	Yes	No
Retiring Participants Can Demand Stock Pursuant To Put Option	Yes, Unless Restricted by By-Laws & Charter Deeming Sponsor to be "Substantially Employee Owned"	No
Participants Vote Their Shares	No, Except in Very Major Issues: Liquidation, Sale, Sale of Substantially All of the Assets, Merger	No, Except in Very Major Issues: Liquidation, Sale, Sale of Substantially All of the Assets, Merger
Tax-Deduction Limit for Combined Qualified Plans	25% of Eligible Compensation, not Counting Dividends paid to ESOP	25% of Eligible Compensation, not Counting Earnings on ESOP Shares

CHAPTER 4

VALUATION CONSIDERATIONS

Why a Valuation Is Needed

The primary regulator of these types of employee benefit plans is the Department of Labor ("DOL"), which draws its authority from the Employee Retirement Income Security Act of 1974 ("ERISA"). ERISA requires that an independent third party appraise the stock in a privately held company owned by an ESOP. Secondarily, the Internal Revenue Service has authority to review the activities of the plan of the deductibility of contributions. The IRS requires a valuation to be performed annually if the plan is leveraged.

Publicly Traded vs. Non-Publicly Traded Companies

Whether or not the employer stock is publicly traded can impact the valuation of the sponsor's stock. Often, banks whose stock is listed on an exchange do not obtain independent valuations as the trustee presumes that the value of the ESOP stock will approximate the market price. However, care should be taken by both the plan sponsor and the trustee to ensure that the use of the bank's "market" price is appropriate.

Guidance on the regulatory definition of publicly traded was issued by the IRS on March 1, 2011 applying Section 401(a)(35) of the Internal Revenue Code to ESOPs. Section 401(a)(35) was issued in 2010 and defined a company as "publicly traded" if the employer stock is traded on either:

+ A national securities exchange that is registered under Section 6 of the Securities and Exchange Act of 1964 (e.g., NYSE or NASDAQ); or

+ A foreign national securities exchange that is officially recognized, sanctioned, or supervised by a governmental authority and where the Security is deemed by the Securities and Exchange Commission as having a ready market (e.g., the FTSE Group All-World Index).

Stock not meeting the definition noted above, which includes stock traded on the over-the-counter bulletin board or the "pink sheets," would not be considered publicly traded and would be required to satisfy the ESOP requirements that apply to non-publicly traded companies. Additionally, the market price of the stock of certain banks, including those meeting the publicly traded definition described above, may be deemed less meaningful after considering factors such as trading volume, free-float, volatility, and other specific factors.

The Appraiser's Client

The trustee of the ESOP is the independent appraiser's client, rather than the bank or bank holding company. Ultimately, the trustee must review and accept the appraiser's opinion.

When a Valuation Is Needed

The ESOP's need for an independent appraisal arises at several points over its life:

+ Initial valuation for the purchase of stock

    • For a new plan, the appraiser may be asked to prepare a preliminary valuation to assess the feasibility and attractiveness of a plan. If a decision is made to proceed, then the appraiser renders an appraisal upon which the transaction occurs.

+ Annual valuation for plan administration purposes

+ Periodic valuation for subsequent transactions

- If a significant transaction affecting the plan sponsor's stock is anticipated to occur, the ESOP trustee may desire assistance from the independent appraiser. The appraiser can analyze the proposed transaction from a financial point of view and may issue a fairness opinion to the ESOP trustee, which may assist the ESOP trustee in voting the shares held by the plan.

+ Upon termination of plan

+ As an informal rule of practice (unsupported by any formal rule), transactions occurring throughout the year occur at the price determined as of the plan's year-end. For example, transactions occurring in calendar year 2012 would occur at the appraised value as of December 31, 2011. However, if certain significant transactions occur in the interim, the ESOP trustee may desire an updated valuation of the stock.

Basic Valuation Concepts

Standards of Value

The *ASA Business Valuation Standards* define the standard of value as "the identification of the type of value being used in a specific engagement; e.g., fair market value, fair value, investment value."[1] The selection of the standard of value drives the application of valuation methods. The most common standards of value include:

+ **Fair Market Value** is the applicable standard of value for ESOP appraisals and is discussed in more detail below;

+ **Statutory Fair Value** is generally defined by judicial interpretation of the relevant statute in a particular state; and,

+ **Fair Value for financial reporting purposes** is defined in Accounting Standards Codification Topic 820 as, "the price that would be received to sell an asset or paid to transfer a liability in an orderly transaction between market participants at the measurement date."[2]

Fair Market Value

Fair market value is the most widely known standard of value and is applicable to almost all federal and state tax valuation matters. Additionally, ERISA defines adequate consideration as, "…in the case of an asset other than a security for which there is a generally recognized market, the fair market value of the asset as determined in good faith by the trustee or named fiduciary…"[3]

Fair market value has been defined in numerous court cases, as well as in Internal Revenue Service Ruling 59-60. Fair market value is defined by the American Society of Appraisers as:

> "The price, expressed in terms of cash equivalents, at which property would change hands between a hypothetical willing and able buyer and a hypothetical willing and able seller, acting at arm's length in an open and unrestricted market, when neither is under compulsion to buy or sell and when both have reasonable knowledge of the relevant facts."[4]

The definition of fair market value presumes the following:

+ **A Willing Seller and a Willing Buyer**. Both are hypothetical parties. Each is assumed to be well-informed about the subject interest and the market context in which it might be transacted.

+ **Arm's Length**. Fair market value assumes willing, financially capable, and informed buyers and sellers, none of whom is related or acting under any compulsion.

+ **Importance of Conditions in Existence at the Valuation Date**. Both internal conditions (financial health of subject bank, credit quality, etc.) and external conditions (state of stock markets, the relevant local, regional, or national economy, and industry conditions) must be determined by investigation and will influence the conclusion of value.

From the point of view of fair market value, these conditions and their future outlook should be assessed as of the specific valuation date.

+ **Focus on the Critical Three - Common Sense, Informed Judgment, and Reasonableness.** Revenue Ruling 59-60 states: "A sound valuation will be based upon all the relevant facts, but the elements of common sense, informed judgment and reasonableness must enter into the process of weighing those facts and determining their aggregate significance."[5]

Levels of Value

Valuation theory suggests that there are three general levels of value applicable to a business or business ownership interest. Many writers parse these ideas more precisely. For purposes of perspective, we define the three traditional levels of value as:

+ **Controlling interest basis** refers to the value of the enterprise as a whole.

+ **Marketable minority interest basis** refers to the value of a minority interest, lacking control, but enjoying the benefit of liquidity as if it were freely tradable in an active market.

+ **Nonmarketable minority interest basis** refers to the value of a minority interest, lacking both control and market liquidity.

The traditional levels of value chart shown on the following page shows the relationship between the three levels of value and demonstrates how the indications of value are obtained at each level of value.

TRADITIONAL LEVELS OF VALUE

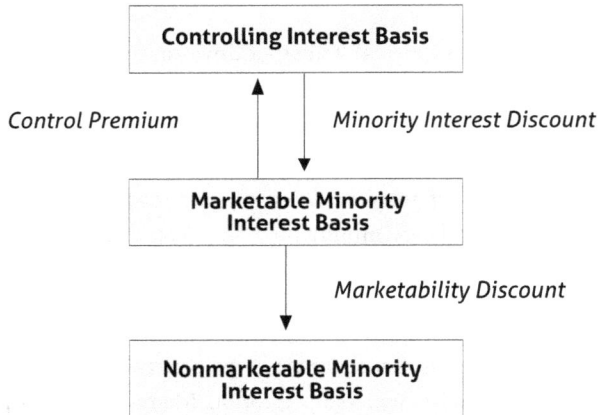

```
          ┌─────────────────────────────────┐
          │     Controlling Interest Basis   │
          └─────────────────────────────────┘
                    ▲          │
   Control Premium  │          │  Minority Interest Discount
                    │          ▼
          ┌─────────────────────────────────┐
          │       Marketable Minority        │
          │         Interest Basis           │
          └─────────────────────────────────┘
                               │
                               │  Marketability Discount
                               ▼
          ┌─────────────────────────────────┐
          │     Nonmarketable Minority       │
          │         Interest Basis           │
          └─────────────────────────────────┘
```

Controlling Interest Level of Value

The highest level of value is called the controlling interest level of value. Controlling interest indications of value are commonly obtained directly by reference to actual change of control transactions using the guideline transactions method, which is described in the discussion of valuation approaches later in this chapter. Additionally, controlling interest indications of value can be obtained indirectly by reference to freely tradable values using a control premium.

The control premium is the difference between the value of a subject interest that exercises control over the company and the value of that same interest lacking control (but enjoying marketability). In practice, the control premium is generally expressed as a percentage of the marketable minority value. When the difference is expressed as a percentage of the controlling interest value, it is referred to as a minority interest discount. Both the concept of the control premium and that of the minority interest discount have been addressed in numerous studies by appraisal professionals and by the various courts.[6]

Many valuation experts further subdivide the controlling interest level of value into strategic control value and financial control value. We define strategic control and financial control as:

+ **Strategic controlling interest basis** refers to the value of the enterprise as a whole, incorporating the strategic intent that may motivate particular buyers and the expected synergies that may result from an acquisition.

+ **Financial controlling interest basis** refers to the value of the enterprise excluding any revenue and expense synergies that may accrue to a strategic buyer. This level of value is viewed from the perspective of a financial buyer, who may expect to benefit by improving the enterprise's cash flow and its capital structure but not through any operating synergies that may be available to a strategic buyer.

If adjusted, the levels of value chart looks like the following:

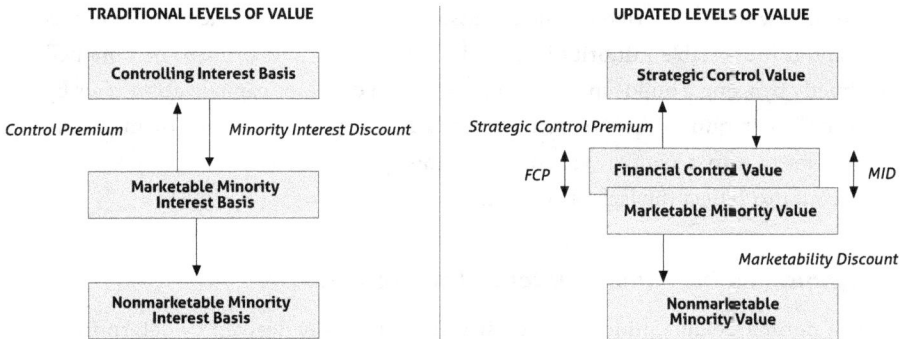

The "FCP" in the right chart is any applicable "financial control premium" over the marketable minority level. The corresponding "MID" is any applicable "minority interest discount." It is widely acknowledged by appraisers that the typical public company pricing is analogous to the financial control level, such that financial control and marketable minority values are often indistinguishable.

Observing the differential between the financial controlling interest level of value and the strategic controlling interest level of value at a specific time in a particular industry can be difficult for a variety of reasons. Generally, a conclusion of value at the strategic controlling interest level of value results in a conclusion of value greater than a conclusion of value at the financial control level. However, a preponderance of financial buyers in a given industry can result in competitive bidding and the acceptance of lower returns by an individual financial buyer, which may increase prices paid by financial buyers to a level comparable to the prices offered and/or paid by strategic buyers.

Marketable Minority Interest Level of Value

The marketable minority interest level of value is typically the reference point for which the other levels are described. Indications of value on a marketable minority interest basis are often obtained by reference to valuation multiples of comparable publicly traded companies using the guideline public company method, which is described in the discussion of valuation approaches later in this chapter. Marketable minority interest indications of value can also be obtained directly by using a build-up methodology, which develops capitalization rates by estimating required rates of return in relation to public markets, or indirectly by reference to a control valuation via the application of a minority interest discount to reflect the lack of control.

Nonmarketable Minority Interest Level of Value

The nonmarketable minority interest value is typically derived by determining value at the marketable minority interest level of value and then applying a discount for lack of marketability. The American Society of Appraisers defines a discount for lack of marketability as "an amount or percentage deducted from the value of an ownership interest to reflect the relative absence of marketability."[7] Thus, a marketable minority interest would be worth more than a nonmarketable minority interest that is identical in all other respects, and the difference between the two (the marketability discount) is due to the inherent risk of holding an illiquid asset. For ESOP appraisals, discounts for lack of marketability generally may be lessened, as many ESOPs contain "put" provisions, requiring the employer or the ESOP itself to repurchase shares of stock from employees.

Valuation Approaches

The process of creating a valuation means consideration of various ways of measuring value. Since Mercer Capital adheres to the *American Society of Appraisers' Business Valuation Standards,* we use its terminology. The ASA recognizes three general approaches to valuation. Within each approach, the appraiser may apply various methods. The valuation methods used are considered by the appraiser to be those most appropriate to the valuation.

Asset Approach

The *ASA BV Standards* define the asset approach as "a general way of determining a value indication of a business, business ownership interest, security, or intangible asset using one or more methods based on the value of the assets net of liabilities."[8] Asset-based valuation methods include those methods that seek to write up (or down) or otherwise adjust the various tangible and/or intangible assets of an enterprise.

Within the asset approach, a potential method used for valuing a financial institution is the net asset value method. The net asset value method develops a valuation indication in the context of a going concern by adjusting the reported book values of a subject bank's assets to their market values and subtracting its liabilities (adjusted to market value, if appropriate). This approach often is less meaningful than the income and market approaches.

Income Approach

The *ASA BV Standards* define the income approach as "a general way of determining a value indication of a business, business ownership interest, security, or intangible asset by using one or more methods through which anticipated benefits are converted into value."[9] Valuation methods under the income approach include those methods that provide for the direct capitalization of earnings estimates, as well as valuation methods calling for the forecasting of future benefits (earnings or cash flows) and then discounting those benefits to the present at an appropriate discount rate. One of the most common methods used to value financial institutions within the income approach is the discounted future benefits method, which relies upon a projection of a future stream of benefits, the present value of which represents the indication of value of the subject bank.

Market Approach

The *ASA BV Standards* define the market approach as "a general way of determining a value indication of a business, business ownership interest, security or intangible asset by using one or more methods that compare the subject to similar businesses, business ownership interests, securities or intangible assets that have been sold."[10]

Within the market approach, the most common methods utilized are:

+ **The Transactions Method**. The transactions method develops an indication of value based upon consideration of actual transactions in the stock of a subject entity. Transactions are reviewed to determine if they have occurred at arm's length, with a reasonable degree of frequency, and within a reasonable period of time relative to the valuation date. Finally, the transactions should be of a similar level of value (i.e., a limited number of transactions involving a small number of shares would generally be inappropriate for a controlling interest valuation). Inferences about current value can sometimes be drawn, even if there is only a limited market for the shares and relatively few transactions occur.

+ **The Guideline Public Company Method**.[11] The guideline public company method develops an indication of value based upon pricing multiples of guideline companies. When valuing banks, guideline companies are most often publicly traded financial institutions that provide a reasonable basis for comparison to the investment characteristics of the subject bank. Sifting through the hundreds of publicly traded banks in the United States, appraisers evaluate comparability on the basis of several measures, most notably asset size, geographic location, asset quality, and profitability. The most commonly used version develops a price/earnings ("P/E") ratio or price/ book value ratio ("P/B") with which to capitalize net income or book value. If the public company group is sufficiently homogeneous with respect to the companies selected and their financial performance, analysts may begin the analysis by calculating an average or median P/E or P/B ratio as representative of the group or subdivide the group by other means. If the analyst determines that certain differences exist between the guideline companies and the subject bank, then the analyst may adjust the median or average multiples to account for these differences. Price/tangible book value ratios frequently are used in addition to or in place of price/reported book value ratios.

+ **The Guidelines Transactions Method.**[12] Also referred to as the merger and acquisition method, the guideline transactions method develops an indication of value based on change of control transactions involving target banks with investment characteristics comparable to the subject bank. Transactions are screened to include only those that occurred within a reasonable period of time proximate to the effective date of the valuation and involve target banks with comparable qualities, including asset size, asset quality, geographic location, and profitability. The most commonly used version develops a P/E or P/B ratio that is used to capitalize net income or book value. Other relevant valuation indicators for the banking industry may include the premium to core deposits.

Hot Topics in ESOP Valuation

Leveraged vs. Unleveraged Transaction

The use of leverage often creates complexity and misunderstanding in a variety of ways. First, if the ESOP's stock purchase is financed with debt, the transaction almost certainly will not create capital immediately, since *American Institute of Certified Public Accountants Statement of Position 93-6* generally does not permit it. This accounting pronouncement should be reviewed with the bank's auditors very carefully before implementing a leveraged plan to avoid any unwelcome adjustments to the holding company's equity. Second, the value of the stock may fall after the leveraged plan is implemented depending upon the treatment of the ESOP debt in the appraisal.

An ESOP can engage in a leveraged transaction involving a minority interest (less than 50% of the outstanding shares) or a controlling interest (more than 50%). When debt is involved, there is the expectation that it will be paid from contributions to the ESOP and possibly distributions (which are made to all shareholders). ESOP appraisers may treat the debt and contributions in a minority interest transaction as an increase in compensation. Hence, costs rise and value falls, with all other things being equal. Value will rise over time as the debt is paid; however, ongoing contributions to the ESOP will continue to reduce earnings. In a control transaction, appraisers may treat the debt as though it were similar to an externally financed stock acquisition. This is appropriate because the controlling shareholder can sell the company and pay the debt. On rare occasions, the debt can be paid from distributions, therefore no reduction in the stock value occurs.

Additionally, the use of leverage can create dilution, which lowers value. Dilution is a reduction in the fair market value per share, which occurs when there is an increase in the number of shares without an immediate, offsetting increase in value due to higher earnings or more capital. In the context of an ESOP, it occurs when: 1) shares are contributed to the plan and a tax deduction is taken for the fair market value of those shares; or, 2) newly issued shares are purchased by the plan and the purchase is financed with debt. Dilution is considered in the determination of fair market value at the time of the appraisal and should not be confused with the decline in value, which sometimes occurs when existing shares are purchased with debt. Dilution is encountered most frequently when a bank is undertaking a new stock offering. The difficulty increases when the ESOP purchases its stock with debt.

Discount for Lack of Marketability

Appraisers often reduce the discount for lack of marketability if the ESOP plan document contains a "put" provision that is legally enforceable and financially viable. The put clause allows the participant to put the stock to the plan, to the employer, or both. An appraiser can apply a different discount for lack of marketability to stock inside an ESOP than to shares outside the plan.

One area of controversy involves the purchase of shares by an ESOP that would otherwise be subject to a larger marketability discount. If the ESOP pays the ESOP appraised value, which is based on a relatively low marketability discount, for shares subject to a larger marketability discount, some have argued that the ESOP would contravene the requirement that it pay no more than fair market value. That is, shareholders outside of the ESOP should not benefit from the put right accorded to ESOP participants.

Repurchase Liability

An emerging liability is the obligation of the plan or the employer to repurchase shares in the plan. The amount of the liability is a function of the value of the stock. Since repurchasing stock takes cash (or capital), the repurchase of shares in a mature ESOP is often in conflict with other financial needs of the business, such as funds needed for expansion. The emerging liability is rarely an issue in new plans and may not be an issue for many years. Appraisers differ as to the treatment of a repurchase liability in appraisals. From bank management's perspective, though, the repurchase liability means that a greater portion of the bank's earnings may be used to redeem shares from ESOP participants exiting the plan, rather than reinvested in the bank. The ESOP repurchase obligation should not be used to reduce unduly the value of the stock and solve the cash flow problem of a mature ESOP.

ENDNOTES

1   American Society of Appraisers, *ASA Business Valuation Standards* ©
     (Revision published November 2009), "Definitions," p 31.

2   ASC 820-10-20 (formerly SFAS 157, paragraph 5).

3   ERISA §1002 (18)(b).

4   American Society of Appraisers, *ASA Business Valuation Standards* ©
     (Revision published November 2009), "Definitions," p 27.

5   IRS Revenue Ruling 59-60.

6   American Society of Appraisers, *ASA Business Valuation Standards* ©
     (Revision published November 2009), "Definitions," p 26.

7   American Society of Appraisers, *ASA Business Valuation Standards* ©
     (Revision published November 2009), "Definitions," p 26.

8   American Society of Appraisers, *ASA Business Valuation Standards* ©
     (Revision published November 2009), "BVS-III Asset-Based Approach to
     Business Valuation," p 9.

9   American Society of Appraisers, *ASA Business Valuation Standards* ©
     (Revision published November 2009), "BVS-IV Income Approach to
     Business Valuation," pp 10-11.

10   American Society of Appraisers, *ASA Business Valuation Standards* ©
     (Revision published November 2009), "BVS-V Market Approach to Business
     Valuation," pp 12-13.

11   American Society of Appraisers, *ASA Business Valuation Standards* ©
     (Revision published November 2009), "SBVS-1 Guideline Public Company
     Method," pp 33-34.

12   American Society of Appraisers, *ASA Business Valuation Standards* ©
     (Revision published November 2009), "SBVS-2 Guideline Transactions
     Method," pp 35-36.

CHAPTER 5

THE ESOP STOCK REPURCHASE OBLIGATION

After implementing an ESOP, the sponsor has an obligation to cash out vested participants when they meet the plan distribution requirements, generally at retirement. Besides obligations due at retirement, there are payouts for death, disability, vested terminations, and the ESOP diversification election.

The chart below depicts an example of this long-term obligation for an ESOP started in 2008 that purchased $8 million of company stock financed over 10 years. The vertical axis measures the annual repurchase obligation. The expected plan repurchases shown in the chart below assume 6% average annual share price appreciation and a positive effect on post-transaction value by the paydown of the ESOP debt.

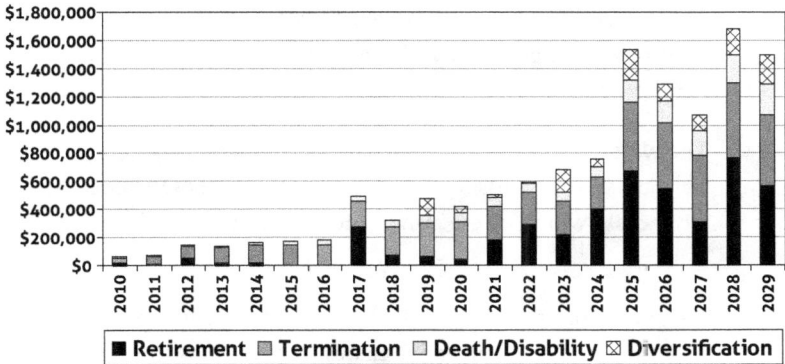

Some of the issues arising for plan sponsors dealing with these long-term, emerging costs are:

+ The obligation is real, but is determined actuarially and is not reflected in the company financials under Generally Accepted Accounting Principles ("GAAP"). There is no requirement to report the obligation under GAAP, even when the repurchase costs are high.

+ Proper ESOP management requires that financial officers understand and manage not just cash flows, but stock flows as well, in light of the requirements of fiduciary prudence to operate the plan for the exclusive benefit of the participants. While there is no guarantee that stock value will rise over time, fiduciaries must show they have acted in the best interests of the participants.

Plan sponsors also must understand the interplay between the repurchase obligation and the major variables affecting the financial health of the plan and its sponsor, such as the following:

+ The independent ESOP stock valuation, which considers the sponsor's earnings capacity that may itself be impacted by the repurchase liability;

+ The ways a bank holding company manages its excess capital (for instance, a possible "sinking fund" for ESOP stock buybacks), which affect value and the resulting buyback liability;

+ The direction of various stock flows, e.g., dilutive new share issues to the plan, repurchases of stock into the plan, or repurchases of stock back into treasury (which can be counter-dilutive to value); and,

+ The plan distribution rules and administrative policies governing the way payments are made to former participants.

A good ESOP repurchase study will help a plan sponsor analyze the many, and sometimes very creative, strategies that can coordinate these variables to keep a plan and its sponsor in the best financial position (and, incidentally, will also represent important documentation of prudence on the part of the fiduciaries). The ESOP repurchase study should not just measure the projected costs arising from the repurchase obligation, but should examine financial strategies for funding and cost containment.

A few central questions to be addressed by fiduciaries (Board of Directors and Trustees) responsible for an ESOP over the long term are:

+   Should the ESOP stock accounts subject the participants to the same risk in their retirement plan as the equity risk for outside stakeholders (as is the case when the ESOP relies entirely on current cash flows or has "buy-sell" funding roughly equivalent to that for other shareholders)?

+   If not, how should the risk be mitigated?

+   How does risk mitigation tie into repurchase funding and prudent fiduciary management of the plan? Reducing risk to ESOP participants implies some funding for the plan liabilities to reduce the risk of impaired payment ability. If there is cash beyond immediate liquidity needs in the plan or on the holding company's balance sheet, then the risk of an account not being paid out is reduced.

Fiduciaries should assess the ESOP repurchase liability within a risk/reward framework. In making decisions on how to use capital, the sponsoring company must balance the competing goals of: 1) supporting the ESOP's liquidity needs and 2) providing capital for the bank's growth. At the extremes, the ESOP could either bear the same risk as non-ESOP shareholders and rely entirely on future cash flow to fund stock purchases, or all the available funds could be directed to supporting the plan, reducing the risk greatly but compromising the bank's growth and capital flexibility.

Since the planning time horizons for ESOP repurchase obligations extend out over a decade and can grow to a relatively large sum, the bulk of the funding will come from current cash flows and the ability to leverage, if the costs grow very large or increase significantly in an given year. Given the long-term nature of the repurchase obligation, a pre-funding strategy can be structured to accumulate sufficient cash to meet short-term obligations. For example, sufficient liquidity can be set aside to cover the largest repurchase obligations expected in several years over the next decade or so.

The following are some basic recommendations for fiduciaries analyzing the repurchase obligation:

+ Fiduciary prudence requires the directors to take steps to measure, fund, and diversify some of the risk inherent in the long term buy-back obligations. Repurchase analyses run for a set of financial and benefit inputs can aid in understanding the sensitivity of the long-term payouts to factors the company can control.

+ To achieve some balance in the competing goals of the ESOP's security and the bank's growth and to demonstrate fiduciary prudence, the Trustees should have their independent appraiser provide some estimates of the effect of various pre-funded amounts for ESOP repurchases on the bank's stock value. No decisions should be made regarding the treatment of the obligation without knowing that approximate range.

+ Coordinate corporate projections with ESOP repurchase studies. Make the valuation firm aware of the anticipated repurchase costs.

+ Do not rely on single-solution financial product providers to address the problem of how to handle the repurchase obligation.

+ Start funding the obligation early in the plan's life, even with just a small amount. Whether the funds are held on the holding company's balance sheet or in the plan depends on a number of factors such as corporate taxes and the age of the plan. Note that you can hold some money in key executive plans, which the executives can receive if the buy-backs are covered, or which can be used to pay the obligations if cash flows are light.

How to Fund the Obligations

The question of how to fund the repurchase obligation is the topic of entire booklets by professional ESOP associations, but we note a few points in this summary of the topic.

+ Contributions of cash to the plan are tax-deductible and generally are sufficient in the early years of an ESOP when attrition of the trust assets due to retirements and other payouts is small. In later years, excess cash in a plan can result in a bleeding ESOP, i.e., an ESOP in which some of the cash in participant accounts is paid out without ever buying a share of stock. To reduce the bleeding ESOP effect, companies with mature ESOPs are often better served by keeping the cash on the balance sheet under corporate control for a variety of reasons – even with the taxation triggered by retaining earnings. The bleeding effect can be exacerbated by IRC §409(p) anti-abuse rules for Subchapter S corporation ESOPs.

+ Cash-efficient, corporately owned life insurance can help with the obligation since payouts to beneficiaries in both of these cases must begin no later than the end of the year following the participant's separation from service. In the interest of ensuring that the policies will stay in force, it is helpful to have a permanent insurance product with cash accumulation that could be accessed to help with buy-back obligations or to pay premiums. Insurance should be owned outside the ESOP, as discussed in detail below.

+ ESOP fiduciaries need to look at planning timeframes extending well beyond a decade for a larger population of plan participants. Once they have taken the essential step of estimating the future liabilities, they have to consider the effect of mortality/morbidity on ESOP payouts – especially for the accounts of highly compensated participants.

+ If there is high anticipated growth in share value, rather than have higher buyback obligations consume more cash, consider setting some cash aside in the near-term for the liability. The cash set-aside could result in lower average annual share price appreciation in future years, especially if the pre-funding was coordinated with a key executive program.

As noted previously, if life insurance is used as a method of helping to fund the ESOP repurchase obligation, the insurance should be held by the sponsoring company rather than by the ESOP. An ESOP can own life insurance, so-called TOLI (Trust Owned Life Insurance). If the ESOP owns the policies, there would be an advantage in:

+ Improved cash flows for the company if the ESOP has the additional cash to invest in the insurance, because of the immediate deductibility of the premiums.

+ The repurchases related to large ESOP accounts are funded in event of death.

However, the drawbacks to ESOP ownership of insurance are quite significant:

+ Some fiduciary issues arise from ESOP ownership of life insurance; for example, ESOP-owned insurance with death benefits or cash for key employees or shareholders could create a possible prohibited transaction.

+ Insurance death benefits paid to the ESOP cannot be used to retire ESOP debt. Current law specifies ESOP loan repayments are to come from annual additions or dividends for that purpose. S corporation ESOPs can use K-1[1] distributions on unallocated shares to retire debt, but the purchase of insurance with them is a gray area.

+ A tax-free death benefit would be paid to a tax-exempt trust.

+ When permanent insurance products are used, there is possible tax-exempt deferred cash value building up in a tax-exempt trust.

+ A large cash infusion from a death benefit will generally repurchase stock for the trust or be paid out to departing participants, which increases the repurchase liability; it is probably better to have the flexibility of a death benefit coming to the balance sheet.

+ The limit for annual contributions to the ESOP must also support payment of the premium(s).

+ Plan fiduciaries must consider the implications of possibly canceling a policy when the death of an insured is a guaranteed benefit to the plan. Younger plan participants may claim fiduciary malfeasance in the elimination of this benefit that would more than likely accrue to them.

Corporately owned insurance contracts, on the other hand, can have numerous benefits:

+ The corporation can use any insurance proceeds or cash values to retire into the treasury as little or as much of the stock as desired, thereby adjusting the issued and outstanding shares, affecting both the size of the ESOP and the future repurchase obligation in light of the financial posture of the company, the plan, and shareholders.

+ The tax-free proceeds from the insurance policy to the company are more flexible than cash in the plan. They can be used to make tax-deductible contributions to the ESOP or loaned to the ESOP to the extent needed. In the case of an internal loan from an insurance benefit or cash values, the company can then make tax-deductible contributions to repay itself. However, the loan would be treated as a reduction in the holding company's equity, as AICPA Statement of Position 93-6 would require the holding company to record a contra-equity equal to the amount of the loan. This contra-equity account, resulting from even the internal loan between company and the ESOP, would decline over time to zero as the loan is repaid.

+   The premium(s) can be made tax-deductible if the company contributes newly issued shares to the plan, which can be adjusted as desired in light of the tax benefits needed and the minimum dilution incurred. If net operating loss carryforwards or other factors mitigate the need for a tax shelter, the company has control of the stock contribution and can choose to make no additional plan contribution.

+   The cash accumulations can be used to fund reasonable discriminatory key executive benefits outside the ESOP to retain critical employees for the benefit of the company and the ESOP participants. The vesting of such accumulated cash to key executives can be linked to the ability of these executives to retire ESOP debt or successfully fund ESOP stock repurchase obligations.

A potential drawback to the corporately owned insurance is:

+   A large tax-free death benefit paid to the corporation could increase the tax liability of the company through alternative minimum tax rules (the company should have its accountant review this possibility and its potential impact on stock valuation).

In short, the significant constraints on trust-owned insurance and the flexibility of a bank with insurance contracts on its balance sheet both argue strongly in favor of having Bank Owned Life Insurance rather than Trust Owned Life Insurance.

When Are ESOP Participants Paid for Their ESOP Accounts?

ESOP benefits are usually paid to participants after their employment with the company ends for any reason. The timing of ESOP benefit payments depends on whether a plan participant is retiring, has died, becomes disabled, or simply is leaving the company. The following IRS and DOL rules apply to the payment of ESOP benefits following a participant's departure from the company:

+ When an ESOP participant retires, becomes disabled, or dies, the ESOP must begin to distribute vested benefits during the plan year following the event. The maximum number of annual installment payments is five.

+ When an ESOP participant's employment terminates for reasons other than retirement, disability, or death, the distribution of his or her ESOP benefits can be delayed, but it must start no later than the sixth plan year after the plan year in which termination occurred (unless the participant is reemployed by the same company before then).

+ ESOP distributions may also be delayed if the ESOP is leveraged, in which case distributions of ESOP-held shares acquired through the loan generally may be delayed until the plan year after the plan year in which the ESOP loan is fully repaid. This does not apply, however, to certain ESOP distributions following the retirement or death of the participant.

+ Rules governing company stock acquired by an ESOP before 1987 differ slightly, and the value of those shares might not be distributed until the participant reaches retirement age

+ The plan must generally begin distributing benefits to an ESOP participant who has reached age 70½ and has not requested an earlier distribution. Payments are made over the participant's life expectancy.[2]

In certain circumstances, participants may receive benefits from the ESOP while they are still employed:

+ Plan participants who are still working (and those who are not) may diversify their account balances if they are age 55 and have been participants for at least 10 years.[3] They have the right during the following five years to diversify up to 25% of company stock that was acquired by the ESOP after December 31, 1986 and that has been allocated to their accounts. During the sixth year, they may diversify up to 50%, less any previously-diversified shares. To satisfy the diversification requirement, the ESOP must: 1) offer at least three alternative investments under either the ESOP or another plan such as a 401(k) plan or 2) distribute cash or company stock to the participants.

+ The employer may choose to pay dividends directly to ESOP participants on company stock allocated to their accounts (usually done by C corporations).

+ The plan must generally begin distributing benefits to an ESOP participant whose allocated shares represent 5% or greater ownership interest in the plan after the participant reaches age 70½, even if the participant is still employed.

+ There are certain other circumstances in which the ESOP plan may provide for in-service distributions, such as after a fixed number of years, upon attainment of a specified age, or upon "hardship."

How Are ESOP Participants Paid for Their ESOP Accounts?

ESOP distributions may be made in substantially equal payments (not less frequently than annually as set by policy) over a period no longer than five years (i.e., six payments over five years). However, this five-year period may be extended an additional year (up to a maximum of five additional years) for each $195,000 or fraction thereof by which a participant's benefit exceeds $985,000 (limits adjusted annually). Distributions are made in the form of cash or stock in a C corporation-sponsored ESOP and cash only in an S corporation-sponsored ESOP.

Please note that these are the most restrictive provisions mandated under current regulation. An employer may pay benefits earlier and must maintain a policy covering distribution guidelines. The policy may be changed prospectively, but all distributions will need to be paid consistently to plan participants and in accordance with regulations, the plan, and policies in place at the time of the distributable event and request for payment. It is not uncommon for these "Administrative Distribution Rules" (which are not part of the ESOP Plan & Trust document) to be adjusted every two or three years to match up with the ability of the sponsor to make the payments and support stock value over time.

ENDNOTES

1   A K-1 return is a tax document used to report the income, losses, and dividends of a business' partners or S corporation shareholders.

2   IRC Section 401(a)(9).

3   IRC Section 401(a)(28)(B).

CHAPTER 6

LEGAL CONSIDERATIONS

Plan Compliance, Record Keeping and Department of Labor Audits

After the implementation of an ESOP, upkeep is needed annually to continue the management of the plan and to keep the plan compliant with the law. For instance, companies that sponsor ESOPs need to perform record keeping each year to allocate shares of company stock to employees and to inform employees of the value of their holdings, based on an independent annual valuation.

For an ESOP, the ongoing compliance process presents unique complexities. Although an ESOP is a qualified, defined-contribution plan, there are significant differences from a 401(k) or profit-sharing plan. The employer and trustees must consider the following to ensure documentation and compliance obligations are met:

+ Plan document amendments as required

+ Summary Plan Description (SPD)

+ Investment policy and actual investment of cash balances

+ Participant education

+ Plan record keeping, including analysis of the census and financial data

+ Production of an allocation report that includes financial statements; summary of financial assumptions and transactions (including release of shares of employer stock) for the plan year; results of applicable compliance tests; participant detail including updated eligibility and vesting; allocation detail in total and per participant including contributions, forfeitures, distributions, dividends or S corporation distributions, investment gain or loss, and ending balances

+ Participant statements

+ Administrative distribution policy

+ Management of the distribution process including Qualified Domestic Relations Orders

+ Method for funding of plan distributions (stock repurchase obligations)

+ Annual IRS Form 5500 tax return series & all related 5500 schedules

+ Plan audit by a CPA for plans with over 100 participants

+ Summary Annual Report (SAR) for participants

Compliance and administration is complex and time consuming. Sponsoring companies should consider retaining professionals to serve as ERISA counsel to prepare document amendments and address other issues, professional record keepers to handle all of the participant details and testing, and a CPA to prepare the Form 5500 tax filing and perform the plan audit (if applicable).

The annual tax return is due by the end of the seventh month after plan year end and is filed with the Department of Labor's Employee Benefits Security Administration (EBSA) in conjunction with the IRS. The DOL uses the filings to determine who will be selected for plan audit by the service.

If an employer's ESOP plan is selected by the DOL for audit, it does not mean there is an anticipated violation. Records will be requested and reviewed over months and a report issued with any findings of error with mandated corrections. ERISA counsel should be contacted upon receiving notification that a plan will be audited. (See Appendix A for a copy of the DOL ESOP Audit Checklist). If there are errors, various remedies are available and will be disclosed by the DOL auditor and resolved.

If an employer is made aware of or discovers an error that is an operational defect and the plan is not being audited by the IRS or DOL, then steps must be taken to correct plan operations and make the plan "whole."

Under an IRS program known as Employee Plans Compliance Resolution System ("EPCRS"), plan sponsors and other plan professionals can correct certain errors in employee retirement plans, in some cases without even having to notify the IRS. Correcting plans in this way allows participants to continue receiving tax-favored retirement benefits and protects the retirement benefits of employees and retirees.

EPCRS includes three levels of correction programs:[1]

+ **The Self-Correction Program (SCP)** permits a plan sponsor to correct "insignificant operational failures" in certain simple plans, such as 403(b) plans, Simplified Employee Pension Plans ("SEPs"), or SIMPLE IRA plans. These corrections can be made without having to notify the IRS and without paying any fee or sanction.

+ **The Voluntary Correction Program (VCP)** allows a plan sponsor, at any time before an audit, to pay a limited fee and receive the IRS's approval for a correction of a qualified plan, a 403(b) plan, SEP, or SIMPLE IRA plan.

+ **The Correction on Audit Program (Audit CAP)** allows a sponsor to correct a failure or an error that has been identified on audit and pay a sanction based on the nature, extent, and severity of the failure being corrected.

The VCP and Audit CAP programs are available to ESOPs. It is recommended that a tax and/or legal professional be involved in the planning of all corrections and filings under the programs.

What Is a Fiduciary?

Generally a fiduciary is anyone who has control or direction over ESOP assets. The principal persons who have a fiduciary role in an ESOP are the members of the Board of Directors and the Trustees of the ESOP, who are appointed by the Board. These fiduciaries are personally liable for their roles in operating the plan for the "exclusive benefit of the participants" under section 404(a)(1) of ERISA.

ESOP Fiduciary Exposure and Fiduciary Liability Coverage

To protect the assets of an ESOP as a qualified plan, plan fiduciaries must be covered by an ERISA bond. The bond coverage amount must be at least 10% of plan assets up to a maximum amount of $1,000,000. This bond protects against liability for potential fund mismanagement by trustees, administrators, and others associated with managing the plan. An ERISA bond is commonly and readily obtained from an insurance company. However, the ERISA bond is not fiduciary liability coverage, which must be more than just "ERISA liability" insurance. The best coverage will encompass any conceivable discretionary judgment action and will not provide for a claims retroactive date.

Fiduciary liability exposure and insurance are at times misunderstood as many employee benefit plan decision-makers expect that there is some insurance coverage within the corporate Commercial and General Liability ("CGL") portfolio that will respond to this exposure. In reality, not only is there no other insurance coverage available, but unlike D&O liability insurance, which almost always carries a specific exclusion for liability arising out of the ERISA legislation, there is no provision for utilization of corporate bylaw indemnification provisions within the liability imposed by ERISA.

There is also confusion with the ERISA-mandated insurance for employee dishonesty, which is satisfied by "ERISA bonds," or more simply an endorsement to existing employee dishonesty insurance coverage. Such coverage has no bearing on any allegations of liability for mismanagement of benefit plan assets, or the decision to utilize a third-party administrator, for example.

Additionally, until recently, large fiduciary liability claims were unheard of, and with the demands of employees relating to benefit plan options, enrollment periods, and continuous changes in individual coverage details, many human resources managers devoted their time to issues other than possible liability scenarios.

Many sellers of liability insurance products do not understand the nuances of ERISA and fiduciary liability insurance. As generalists, many otherwise well-qualified agents do not have the resources to devote to getting involved with coverage details of fiduciary liability insurance. As a result, many organizations purchase and maintain relatively low limits, without detailed thought toward limits benchmarking or individual employer exposure.

For many employers fiduciary liability insurance remains much of a mystery, with respect to both exposure and appropriate insurance coverage. The complexities and impending changes of the ERISA legislation continue to compound the liability exposure of corporate executives, many of whom remain unaware of their exposures as well as the exposure of their personal assets in this liability.

The good news is that there are specialty insurers working in the area of ESOP fiduciary liability insurance in sufficient numbers to get competitive quotes for the required coverage. ESOP sponsors should take care to review the terms of their CGL coverage.

Some Basic Bank Regulatory Considerations

When considering the purchase of bank or bank holding company stock by an ESOP, attention must be given to the possible application bank regulatory provisions such as Regulation W of the Federal Reserve ("Reg. W") and the change of control provisions of the 1956 Bank Holding Company Act ("BHCA") in addition to the provisions of the Internal Revenue Code applicable to such plans.

In most instances, a bank holding company will serve as the sponsor of the ESOP with the bank subsidiary also serving as an adopting employer thereby covering the employees of the bank. To fund the Plan, the bank would "upstream" funds in the form of a dividend or make direct contributions to the ESOP based upon the compensation of its employees. These contributions would be utilized to purchase stock in the bank holding company.

In some cases, however, the bank may be the sponsor of the ESOP for state tax reasons or the absence of a bank holding company.

In general, Reg. W governs transactions between member banks and their affiliates such as a purchase of assets from an affiliate, extension of credit to an affiliate, investment in securities offered by an affiliate, issuance of a guarantee on behalf of an affiliate and certain other transactions that expose a member bank to its affiliate's credit or investment risk. For purposes of applying the provisions of Reg. W, an ESOP may be considered to be an "affiliate" relative to the acquisition of stock of a bank. However, Reg. W would not apply to a bank holding company that carries out these transactions with the ESOP as its affiliate.

For purposes of applying the change of control rules, even a minority interest ESOP may need to demonstrate that it is not in "control" of the bank, as defined in the BHCA or the ESOP may be deemed to be a bank holding company itself.

To avoid what is deemed a "change of control" for a member bank or its holding company sponsoring an ESOP, the trustees of the ESOP will often agree that the plan will not acquire 25% or more of the voting stock or in any way gain control without prior approval from the Federal Reserve. The ESOP is required to play a passive role if the Plan is to own from 10% to less than 25% of the voting shares. The passivity commitments may include, among others, an agreement not to seek to exercise a controlling influence over management or policies of the bank, and an agreement not to seek or accept representation on the board of directors. An ESOP transaction can be structured to avoid the characterization of control.

Other required agreements pertaining to the ESOP's ability to acquire securities include:

+ The ESOP will not acquire any security prohibited to the holding company by the BHCA;

+ The ESOP will not take on debt that results in the combined debt of the holding company and the ESOP exceeding 30% of the holding company equity without Federal Reserve approval;

+ If the ESOP is to acquire greater than 25% of a holding company's shares or if counter-dilution could result in an increase in the ESOP's ownership interest to that level, prior approval must be obtained to be a registered bank holding company.

Although the passivity commitments were developed by the Federal Reserve in the context of bank holding company regulation, these principles are of general applicability to investments in nonmember banks and national banks presently regulated by the FDIC and the OCC, respectively, and eventually to be regulated by the FDIC in the case of state chartered savings institutions and by the OCC in the case of federally chartered savings institutions.

What Securities Can an ESOP Purchase?

The simplest and most general rule is that an ESOP must own the employer security with the highest and best voting rights and dividend preferences.[2]

The technical definition of "employer securities" means common stock issued by the employer (or by a corporation that is a member of the same controlled group) having a combination of voting power and dividend rights equal to or in excess of:

+ That class of common stock of the employer having the greatest voting power; and,

+ That class of common stock of the employer having the greatest dividend rights.

An ESOP sponsored by an S corporation must hold the single class of stock required of S corporations. This is the common voting stock, even though some S corporations have both voting and non-voting shares (which are not treated as two "classes" of stock), the ESOP cannot buy non-voting equity.

Many S corporations, in becoming an ESOP company, will recapitalize some or all of the non-voting shares with voting shares, which are then sold to the ESOP. This is occasionally the case when using an ESOP to consolidate a number of minority, non-voting equity interests into a single untaxed shareholder (the ESOP).

Closely held C corporations often have multiple classes of stock and hundreds of shareholders. This is an area where a good securities counsel with knowledge of ESOP law is essential. A discussion of the many alternatives of stock that may be issued to the ESOP is beyond the scope of this handbook, but an example will illustrate a few possibilities.

A C corporation ESOP can own a convertible preferred stock with voting rights instead of common voting shares. This would mean that the preferred dividend could be paid only on the ESOP shares, and not on shares held outside the ESOP (if not required on the common voting stock, for example). Dividends characterized as reasonable by the IRS would be deductible to the C corporation sponsor if used to retire ESOP stock acquisition debt. Further, the conversion of the preferred stock to common stock at the full curtailment of the ESOP loan can result in the ESOP ownership decreasing as a percentage of the common equity and the non-ESOP ownership increasing by virtue of the indirect equity kicker.

Another factor to keep in mind is the ability of bank holding companies to both sponsor an ESOP and effect corporate redemptions of their shares. This opens up the option of providing a tax-shield for the purchase of classes of stock that the ESOP cannot purchase directly. The holding company redemption of shares ineligible for ESOP purchases is followed by the reissuance of new common voting shares to the plan in an amount sufficient to offset the tax consequences of the non-deductible stock redemption.

ENDNOTES

1   EPRC IRS Overview: http://mer.cr/o8GF1h.

2   IRC 409(l).

CHAPTER 7

ESOP INSTALLATION CONSIDERATIONS

Dos and Don'ts When Installing a Plan

Do:

+ Coordinate the ESOP design with all compensation, employee benefit, key executive plan, and capitalization requirements. This coordination can at times even include a major stockholder's estate plan.

+ Consider using an ESOP to assist in repaying TARP or SBLF obligations, potentially in conjunction with other capital raising alternatives.

+ Ensure that the bank has sufficient profitability to take advantage of the tax advantages of contributions to an ESOP.

+ Educate employees regarding their influence on the value being created in the ESOP's stockholdings.

+ Engage in the process of managing the interaction and effect of stock flows between the company, shareholders, and ESOP.

+ Consider the funding requirements for the ESOP's ongoing stock repurchase obligations and actively manage the balance between the emerging liability and the bank's financial needs.

+ Obtain independent appraisals of the fair market value of closely held or thinly traded stock for the implementation of the ESOP and for ongoing ESOP transactions.

Don't:

+   Implement an ESOP without discussing the complex issues around plan design with a team of experienced professionals.

Managing the Implementation Process

Implementing a new ESOP prompts many questions, and the plan's investment in employer securities creates a different level of complexity than that found in the typical 401(k) or IRA. As such, expert advice is often needed from a variety of parties to resolve a number of issues. We have detailed a few key steps as well as some key questions to consider for certain steps to assist with successfully managing the implementation of an ESOP.

+   Examine strategic alternatives for the bank and determine whether an ESOP is an attractive option.

    •   What are the strategic goals of the bank? Will an ESOP assist and/or complement the bank's strategic objectives?

    •   What are the primary goals and objectives for the ESOP? To attract, retain, award employees? To improve capitalization? To assist with repayment of TARP and/ or SBLF obligations? To provide an exit strategy for a shareholder?

    •   What are the potential drawbacks to an ESOP?

    •   How does an ESOP compare to other strategic alternatives?

+   Gauge interest among stakeholders (senior managers, shareholders, board, and employees) for installing an ESOP.

+   Engage a financial advisor to conduct a feasibility study, which typically provides a baseline estimate of the bank's value for the Board and management to consider when determining the attractiveness of the plan.

- Does the financial advisor have the appropriate expertise, (credentials, banking industry expertise, ESOP experience, etc.)? Is the financial advisor independent?

+ Engage an ERISA attorney and plan administrator to discuss plan design.

    - Do these professionals have the appropriate expertise (credentials, banking industry expertise, ESOP experience, etc.)? Are they independent?

+ Decide whether or not to proceed with the transaction.

+ Determine the transaction structure.

    - How much stock will be transacted?

    - Whose stock will be purchased by the ESOP? Will the stock be newly issued and/or purchased from an existing shareholder?

+ Determine the funding mechanism.

    - Will the plan be leveraged, non-leveraged, or some combination?

    - Who will provide the loan if the plan is leveraged? What will the terms of the debt be?

    - How will the additional leverage impact the bank's value (both at implementation and going forward) and financial condition (earnings and balance sheet/capital ratio impact)?

+ Determine ESOP trustee or Administrative Committee.

    - Will these roles be filled internally (from an officer or group of employees within the company) or outside the company (attorney or corporate trustee)?

+ Determine the strategy, depth, and breadth of employee communications once implemented.

+ Engage a financial advisor to render an appraisal upon which the transaction can occur.

+ Discuss the treatment of emerging liability created by the ESOP's obligation to repurchase shares once the plan is implemented with your team of advisors.

+ Formalize ESOP documents and necessary filings.

+ Close the transaction.

Selection of the Advisory Team and Their Roles

Perhaps the most important aspect to successfully implementing an ESOP is to assemble a collegial and competent team. Banking industry and ESOP expertise should be an important consideration when selecting your advisors. Employee benefit plan design and administration is complex and requires the services of a number of professionals.

+ **Trustee** – The trustee acts as a fiduciary for the best interest of the plan participant and may be very active in an ESOP. In the context of an ESOP, the trustee is responsible for the purchase of employer securities and the proper maintenance and administration of the plan. When dealing with closely held securities, the trustee has a heightened level of responsibility. With respect to any plan which requires an appraisal, the trustee must select the appraiser and approve the conclusion of value for securities held by the plan.

+ **Administrator** – The administrator is responsible for record keeping and may also assist with tax filings and maintenance of plan documents. It is best not to handle the annual plan administration in-house. Engage a third party ESOP administrative specialty firm to prepare the annual trust reconciliation and accounting, the participant account statements, and the filing of the Form 5500 tax return for the plan.

+ **Plan Sponsor** – The plan sponsor is typically the company.

+ **Administrative Committee** – Known by a variety of names, an administrative committee is often formed to assist the plan administrator and trustee with various duties associated with the routine administration of the plan.

+ **Attorney or Plan Designer** – The attorney works with the plan sponsor, administrative committee, and trustee to design the plan and create the documents necessary to implement it. Choose a design and implementation advisor who will work: a) with your CPA, corporate counsel, and other existing advisors, and b) under a capped fee arrangement – preferably in stages, with at least a cutoff point after a discovery phase.

+ **Financial Advisor** – The financial advisor may assist the trustee in determining the feasibility of a plan or the fairness of transactions engaged in by the plan from a financial point of view.

+ **Appraiser** – The appraiser provides the independent appraisals necessary to implement and administer the plan. (See Chapter 4, which discusses the scope of work by the appraiser. The use of the term "appraisal" is very specific in this context.)

Assure good communications between your corporate operations, the independent valuation firm, and the plan administrator. Be prepared to deal with complexity and be part of the process. This process has saved many shareholders and companies millions in taxes, made a controlled market for the stock, and rewarded the loyal, long term employees generously.

DEPARTMENT OF LABOR ESOP AUDIT CHECKLIST

1. ☐ The Plan's Annual Report (Form 5500), including the audited financial statements and the independent auditor's opinion thereon.

2. ☐ The current Plan document including any and all amendments.

3. ☐ The current trust agreement for the Plan.

4. ☐ The current Adoption agreement including any amendments.

5. ☐ The Summary Plan Description as distributed to participants in the Plan.

6. ☐ The most recent I.R.S. qualification letter for the Plan.

7. ☐ The Plan's Summary Annual Reports as distributed to participants for the last three consecutive years.

8. ☐ Financial statements, canceled checks, wire transfer statements, and other documents revealing the Company's contribution to the plan.

9. ☐ The Plan's current fidelity bond policy (which identifies the Plan as the named insured, the bond carries no deductible, the amount is sufficient to meet ERISA requirements, and that the general policy provisions include a one year discovery period).

10. ☐ The Trustees and Plan Administrator's fiduciary liability insurance policy(ies) (if applicable).

11. ☐ The Plan's written investment policies/guidelines (if applicable).

12. ☐ Information pertaining to the Plan's purchase of Company shares. Such information should include:

   A. ☐ The characteristics of the Company shares (i.e. common stock, preferred stock, cumulative preferred stock, participating preferred stock, stock warrants, stock restrictions, voting, non-voting, etc.);

   B. ☐ The date(s) that the Plan purchased the aforementioned shares;

   C. ☐ The price paid by the Plan for the Company Stock;

   D. ☐ The independent appraisals used by the Plan's fiduciaries to ascertain that the Plan was purchasing the party-in-interest investments at an arm's length price;

   E. ☐ The price paid for the aforementioned independent appraisals;

   F. ☐ The identification of those assets liquidated by the Plan in order to purchase this investment (if applicable);

   G. ☐ The identity of the broker(s) transferring the company stock [if applicable];

   H. ☐ Document any fees and/or commissions paid by the Plan in purchasing and transferring the stock to the Plan;

   I. ☐ If debt was incurred to purchase the employer shares, and this debt remains outstanding, please provide the allocation formula and accompanying work product used by the Plan fiduciaries to release these encumbered shares to the Plan participants in accordance with D.O.L. Reg. §2550.408b-3(h). This information should include the Plan's amortization schedule; a schedule of payments made to date; a schedule illustrating the appropriate release of encumbered shares to the Plan's trust account once payment was received; and, the allocation of the encumbered shares to the participants' individual accounts.

13. ☐ Information pertaining to the Plan's continued holding of Company stock. Such information should include:

A. ☐ The Plan's rate of return on this party-in-interest investment;

B. ☐ Dividends paid by the Company to the Plan;

C. ☐ Sales of the party-in-interest Company stock from the Plan; to include, but not be limited to, the following information:

1. ☐ the date the shares were sold;

2. ☐ the identification of the purchaser;

3. ☐ the purchase price paid for the shares;

4. ☐ the method used by the Plan's fiduciaries to determine the purchase price;

5. ☐ the identification of any fees and/or commissions paid by the Plan in the selling of the shares; and

6. ☐ the identification of those parties who received fees and/or commissions from the sales of these party-in-interest investments;

14. ☐ Provide a list of all Company employees; indicate current employees, also provide the date and reason former employees terminated such as retirement, disability, death or termination for some other reason.

15. ☐ For each terminated person identified in item #13, indicate whether that person received a distribution from the Plan, indicate whether the person elected to receive cash or Company stock, indicate the date the person was given a distribution, also provide the dollar ($) amount of the distribution.

16. ☐ For each terminated person identified in item # 13, indicate whether that person exercised a put option, submit a copy of the put option exercised, the total value of the put option at the time it was exercised (# of shares and dollar per share), and the determination of the value of the security at the time it was exercised, payment terms and schedules.

17. ☐ Provide a list of all hardship distributions made from the Plan; provide a copy of the documentation submitted requesting the hardship distributions and the review and approval process, also indicate the amount and date of each hardship distribution.

18. ☐ Management letters written to the Plan's fiduciaries from the Plan's independent certified public accounting firm.

19. ☐ Management letters written to the Company's Board of Directors from the Company's independent certified public accounting firm.

20. ☐ Information pertaining to any private placement or private sale of Company stock for the past three years (if applicable).

21. ☐ The Company share certificates owned by the Plan and the percentage of outstanding Company shares held by the Plan.

22. ☐ A list of current Company shareholders and the number of shares that they own.

23. ☐ Company dividend policies on the stock held by the Plan.

24. ☐ A list of all Company mergers within the last three years that required shareholder vote.

25. ☐ A list of all Company consolidations within the last three years that required shareholder vote.

26. ☐ A list of all Company recapitalizations within the last three years that required shareholder vote

27. ☐ A list of all Company reclassifications within the last three years that required shareholder vote.

28. ☐ A list of all Company liquidations within the last three years that required shareholder vote.

29. ☐ A list of all Company dissolutions within the last three years that required shareholder vote.

30. ☐ A list of all sales of the Company or portions of the Company within the last three years that required shareholder vote.

31. ☐ A list of Company officers and Plan Trustees for Plan.

About the Authors

CORPORATE CAPITAL RESOURCES, LLC

www.ccrva.com | 540.345.4190

W. William Gust, J.D., LLM

bill_gust@ccrva.com

Bill Gust has been assisting closely held corporations in developing and integrating business succession and estate plans for over 20 years. As part of the process, Bill works closely with allied professionals in banking, insurance and financial services industries. The development of a successful business succession strategy requires the integration of multiple disciplines to properly implement life insurance, deferred compensation, and estate planning strategies necessary for a tax-favored transition.

Bill serves as the President of Corporate Capital Resources, a wholly owned subsidiary of the Roanoke law firm Gentry Locke Rakes & Moore. In addition to his consulting role on behalf of Corporate Capital Resources, Bill is a Partner in Gentry Locke Rakes & Moore, where he specializes in Business, Tax, and Estate Planning.

Michael A. Coffey

michael_coffey@ccrva.com

Michael Coffey is a managing vice president of Corporate Capital Resources, responsible for structuring stock transactions and key executive benefit packages. He has been instrumental in structuring over $200 million in stock sales, transfers, and gifts for the owners of closely held corporations to family, key employees, and public/private charitable concerns. His work over the past 15 years has focused on tax-favored transactions for business continuity, estate plans for private shareholders and their families, as well as charitable gifts.

As a member of The National Center for Employee Ownership and the ESOP Association, Michael has published numerous articles on employee ownership issues, and has addressed many national forums on tax-advantaged business perpetuation.

Lisa J. Tilley, CPA

lisa_tilley@ccrva.com

Lisa Tilley is a Certified Public Accountant who has been assisting closely held corporations in developing and administering employee benefit programs, as well as assisting them with business succession planning for over 20 years. Lisa works closely with her client's team of professionals in law, banking, insurance, and financial services to ensure coordination of efforts and completion of goals. The development of a successful business succession plan requires the integration of multiple disciplines to properly implement life insurance, deferred compensation and estate planning strategies necessary for a tax favored transition. Lisa also serves as a resource to clients on a continuing basis after transition begins by educating new managers and consulting in matters such as cash flow, share price management, and employee incentives.

Lisa serves as Senior Management Consultant of Corporate Capital Resources, LLC, a wholly owned subsidiary of the Roanoke law firm Gentry Locke Rakes & Moore, LLP. In addition to her consulting role on behalf of Corporate Capital Resources, Lisa is past President of the Roanoke Area Chapter of the Virginia Society of CPAs, a member of the American Institute of CPAs, is an Alumnus of Leadership Roanoke Valley and a founding member of the Women's Professional Leadership Network.

MERCER CAPITAL

www.mercercapital.com | 901.685.2120

Andrew K. Gibbs, CFA, CPA/ABV

gibbsa@mercercapital.com

Andy Gibbs leads Mercer Capital's Financial Institutions Group.

Andy provides valuation and corporate advisory services to financial institutions for purposes including ESOPs, mergers and acquisitions, profit sharing plans, estate and gift tax planning, compliance matters, and corporate planning.

Andy has extensive experience working with financial institutions in merger and acquisition advisory engagements. He has assisted buyers in evaluating the attractiveness of acquisition candidates, determining a price for the target institution, structuring the transaction, and evaluating different forms of financing. For sell-side clients, Andy has analyzed the potential value that the institution may receive upon a sale, assisted in locating potential buyers, and participated in negotiating a final transaction price and merger agreement.

In addition, Andy directs projects related to the valuation of intangible assets under Accounting Standards Codification ("ASC") 805 and impairment testing under ASC 350.

Andy is the co-author of *The Bank Director's Valuation Handbook: What Every Director Must Know About Valuation*, with Jay D. Wilson, Jr., CFA, as well as *Acquiring a Failed Bank: A Guide to Understanding, Valuing, and Accounting for Transactions in a Distressed Environment*, published by Peabody Publishing, LP.

Jay D. Wilson, Jr., CFA

wilsonj@mercercapital.com

Jay Wilson is a vice president and a senior member of Mercer Capital's Financial Institutions Group.

Jay is involved in the valuation of financial institutions for purposes including ESOPs, mergers and acquisitions, profit sharing plans, estate and gift tax planning, compliance matters, and corporate planning.

Jay has extensive experience providing public and private clients with fair value opinions and related assistance pertaining to goodwill and intangible assets, stock-based compensation, loan portfolios, and other financial assets and liabilities. Jay also directs projects in a litigated context, including tax disputes, dissenting shareholder actions, and ESOP related matters.

Jay is a co-author of *The Bank Director's Valuation Handbook: What Every Director Must Know About Valuation*, with Andrew K. Gibbs, CFA, CPA/ABV, and *Acquiring a Failed Bank: A Guide to Understanding, Valuing, and Accounting for Transactions in a Distressed Environment*, published by Peabody Publishing, LP.

Madeleine C. Gilman

gilmanm@mercercapital.com

Madeleine Gilman is a senior member of Mercer Capital's Financial Institutions Group. Maddie is involved in the valuation of financial institutions, ESOPs, corporate entities, as well as valuation for estate and gift tax planning matters.

Maddie has extensive experience providing public and private clients with fair value opinions and related assistance pertaining to goodwill and intangible assets, stock-based compensation, loan portfolios, and other financial assets and liabilities.

Maddie is a contributing author to *The Bank Director's Valuation Handbook: What Every Director Must Know About Valuation*, as well as *Acquiring a Failed Bank: A Guide to Understanding, Valuing, and Accounting for Transactions in a Distressed Environment*, published by Peabody Publishing, LP.

About Corporate Capital Resources, LLC

Corporate Capital Resources works with clients involved in a variety of activities ranging from banking and service to manufacturing and sales. Our customers also range significantly in size, from a handful of employees at a closely held family company to companies with locations in several states.

Possibilities - How We Help Our Clients

+ **Banking & Lending** – Money is the lifeblood of a business. Helping companies secure capital needed for growth often requires extensive expertise in defining assets and demonstrating ability to repay. We have the ability to help companies present compelling cases for growth and the contacts with the banking industry to realize capital.

+ **Business Continuity** – How can you effectively plan to pass ownership to a new generation? The needs of both ownership and the company must be balanced to create an optimum environment for potential success. Corporate Capital Resources has effectively helped transition ownership to both individuals and employee owners. We help ensure the transition of your business with minimal adverse tax effects. The ultimate goal is best summarized in three concepts for private shareholders: control, flexibility, and financial efficiency.

+ **Business Consulting** – We can work creatively with your existing tax or legal counsel to help you address any number of problems that often limit growth, including taxation, cash flow, and financial management issues.

For more information, visit our website at www.ccrva.com, or contact Bill Gust or Michael Coffey at 540.345.4190.

About Mercer Capital

The Financial Institutions Group of Mercer Capital provides a broad range of specialized valuation and advisory services to the financial services industry. Though maintaining a particular emphasis among commercial banks, the Financial Institutions Group also assists insurance services, specialized finance companies, mortgage bankers, asset managers, broker/dealers, and merchant processors.

Mercer Capital has been assisting financial institutions with significant corporate valuation, transactions, and other strategic decisions for 30 years. We have provided hundreds of sound, well-documented financial analyses and valuation opinions for financial institutions large and small. In addition, we have a wealth of transaction experience helping clients with mergers, acquisitions, recapitalizations, and other substantial transactions.

Mercer Capital is a thought-leader among valuation firms in the financial institutions industry. In addition to scores of articles and three books - *Acquiring a Failed Bank* (2010), *The Bank Director's Valuation Handbook* (2009), and *Valuing Financial Institutions* (1991) - the Financial Institutions Group publishes *Bank Watch*, a free monthly e-mail newsletter covering five U.S. regions.

Mercer Capital's Financial Institutions Valuation Services

+ Bank and Financial Institution Valuation
+ Bank ESOP Valuations
+ Loan Portfolio Valuation
+ Valuation for Financial Reporting
+ Goodwill Impairment Testing
+ Valuation for Tax Compliance
+ Transaction Advisory Consulting
+ Capital Raising Consulting

For more information, visit our website at www.mercercapital.com, or contact Andy Gibbs or Jay Wilson at 901.685.2120.

www.ingramcontent.com/pod-product-compliance
Lightning Source LLC
Chambersburg PA
CBHW061837220326
41599CB00027B/5316